# PERSPECTIVES

## ON FAMILY MINISTRY

## BOOKS IN THIS SERIES

*Perspectives on Children's Spiritual Formation: Four Views,* ed. Michael Anthony; contributors: Greg Carlson, Tim Ellis, Trisha Graves, Scottie May

*Perspectives on Christian Worship: Five Views,* ed. J. Matthew Pinson; contributors: Ligon Duncan, Dan Kimball, Michael Lawrence and Mark Dever, Timothy Quill, Dan Wilt

*Perspectives on Church Government: Five Views,* ed. R. Stanton Norman and Chad Brand; contributors: Daniel Akin, James Garrett, Robert Reymond, James White, Paul Zahl

*Perspectives on the Doctrine of God: Four Views,* ed. Bruce A. Ware; contributors: Paul Helm, Robert E. Olson, John Sanders, Bruce A. Ware

*Perspectives on Family Ministry: Three Views,* ed. Timothy Paul Jones, contributors: Timothy Paul Jones, Paul Renfro, Brandon Shields, Randy Stinson, Jay Strother

*Perspectives on Election: Five Views,* ed. Chad Brand; contributors: Jack W. Cottrell, Clark Pinnock, Robert L. Reymond, Thomas B. Talbott, Bruce A. Ware

*Perspectives on Your Child's Education: Four Views,* ed. Timothy Paul Jones; contributors: Mark Eckel, G. Tyler Fischer, Timothy Paul Jones, Troy Temple, Michael S. Wilder

*Perspectives on the Ending of Mark: Four Views,* ed. David Alan Black; contributors: Darrell Bock, Keith Elliott, Maurice Robinson, Daniel Wallace

*Perspectives on Spirit Baptism: Five Views,* ed. Chad Brand; contributors: Ralph Del Colle, H. Ray Dunning, Larry Hart, Stanley Horton, Walter Kaiser Jr.

Leonard G. Goss, Series Editor

# PERSPECTIVES
## ON FAMILY MINISTRY
### 3 VIEWS

PAUL RENFRO

BRANDON SHIELDS · JAY STROTHER

FOREWORD BY RANDY STINSON

EDITED BY TIMOTHY PAUL JONES

B&H
ACADEMIC

NASHVILLE, TENNESSEE

Perspectives on Family Ministry

ISBN: 978-0-8054-4845-0


Published by B&H Publishing Group
Nashville, Tennessee



Dewey Decimal Classification: 259.1
Subject Heading: MINISTRY \ CHURCH WORK WITH FAMILIES


Scripture quotations are taken from the *Holman Christian Standard Bible* ® Copyright © 1999, 2000, 2002, 2003 by Holman Bible Publishers. Used by permission.


Printed in the United States of America

12 13 14 15 16 • 21 20 19 18 17
VP

Dedicated to our parents

*J. Darrell and Patricia Jones*

*LeCreath and Burta Renfro*

*Jim and Lisa Shields*

*Ralph and Barbara Stinson*

*Greg and Paula Strother*

# Contents

Contributors                                                              ix
Acknowledgments                                                           xi
Foreword                                                                   1

**Part 1   Why Every Church Needs Family Ministry**

Chapter 1 — Confessions of a Well-Meaning Youth Minister        6

Chapter 2 — The Task Too Significant to Hire Someone
            Else to Do                                                    15

Chapter 3 — Historical Contexts for Family Ministry           26

Chapter 4 — Foundations for Family Ministry                   37

**Part 2   How Churches Are Doing Family Ministry**

Chapter 5 — Family-Integrated Ministry: Family-Driven Faith   54

Chapter 6 — Responses to Paul Renfro                          79

Chapter 7 — Family-Based Ministry: Separated Contexts,
            Shared Focus                                                  98

Chapter 8 — Responses to Brandon Shields                     121

Chapter 9 — Family-Equipping Ministry: Church and
            Home as Cochampions                                          140

Chapter 10 — Responses to Jay Strother                       168

Author Index                                                             186
Subject Index                                                            190
Scripture Index                                                          194

# Contributors

*Timothy Paul Jones* has authored, coauthored, or edited more than a dozen books, including *Conspiracies and the Cross, Misquoting Truth, Christian History Made Easy,* and the best seller *The Da Vinci Codebreaker*. After fourteen years in vocational ministry, including eight years at First Baptist Church of Rolling Hills in the Tulsa metropolitan area, Timothy now serves as associate professor of leadership and church ministry at The Southern Baptist Theological Seminary in Louisville, Kentucky. In addition to receiving the bachelor of arts in biblical studies from Manhattan Christian College and the master of divinity from Midwestern Baptist Theological Seminary, Timothy has earned the doctor of philosophy from Southern Seminary. His academic research has earned the Scholastic Recognition Award from the North American Professors of Christian Education as well as the Baker Book House Award for theological studies. Timothy, his wife Rayann, and their daughter Hannah reside in the city of St. Matthews, near Louisville, Kentucky.

*Paul Renfro* is one of the pastors at Grace Family Baptist Church, a family-integrated church in Spring, Texas. He gives leadership to the church's discipleship ministry with a special emphasis on equipping men to shepherd their families. He is also the director of the Alliance for Church and Family Reformation, an organization committed to promoting family discipleship, family integration within traditional structures, and family-integrated churches. Paul has served as a pastor, a singles minister, a teacher in both public and private schools, the headmaster of a classical Christian school, and a church planter. He received his master's degree from Southwestern Baptist Theological

Seminary. Paul is married to his wife Laurie, and together they home-educate their four children: Josh, Brianne, Jenna, and Daniel.

*Brandon Shields* oversees high school and collegiate ministries at Highview Baptist Church, a multisite megachurch with six campuses in north central Kentucky and southern Indiana. Brandon has served in youth ministry for almost ten years. He recently earned the doctor of philosophy from The Southern Baptist Theological Seminary, where he conducted research on youth ministry retention and dropout rates. Brandon is married to Emily, and they have two children, James and Cooper.

*Randy Stinson* serves as president of the Council for Biblical Manhood and Womanhood (CBMW) and as dean of the School of Leadership and Church Ministry at The Southern Baptist Theological Seminary in Louisville, Kentucky. After sensing God's call into the ministry, Randy earned degrees from Southeastern Baptist Theological Seminary (M.Div.) and The Southern Baptist Theological Seminary (Th.M. and Ph.D.). He served as a local church pastor for ten years and for seven years as executive director of CBMW. Randy and his wife, Danna, worship at Highview Baptist Church with their six children: Gunnar, Georgia, Fisher, Eden, Payton, and Willa.

*Jay Strother* is the emerging generations minister at Brentwood Baptist Church, in the Nashville area, where he and the emerging generations team partner with parents to guide Christian growth in three thousand families. He has worked with students, children, and their parents since he was nineteen years old. Jay graduated from Greenville College with the bachelor of science degree in secondary education and the social sciences. He has also earned the master of divinity from New Orleans Baptist Theological Seminary. For three years he wrote a monthly feature for *Living with Teenagers* magazine, and he has authored four small-group studies for Serendipity House, including *Canvas: Mystery* and the upcoming *Small Group Life: Formation*. His favorite stories come from the adventures of life with his wife, Tanya, and their three lively little girls, Eliza, Lexi, and Ella. Jay enjoys good books, good coffee, and St. Louis Cardinals baseball.

# Acknowledgments

I didn't know it at the time, but this book began several years ago in a doctoral seminar with Dr. Mark Senter III. In that seminar my studies in the history of youth ministry combined with my experiences in student ministry to reveal a missing element in the Christian formation of youth and children: *family discipleship*. This revelation resulted in a number of revisions in my ministry perspectives and practices. After I became a professor at The Southern Baptist Theological Seminary, these revisions grew into a renewed understanding of how the church and Christian family ought to relate to each other.

Now, my work as a pastor and a professor has birthed this book, a book that represents not only my efforts and the work of the contributors but also the efforts of many persons whose names do not appear in the list of contributors. Mike Nappa of Nappaland Literary Agency moved this project from an ephemeral idea to a well-focused proposal. Telephone and e-mail conversations with Michelle Anthony, Voddie Baucham, Jim Burns, Mark DeVries, John Erwin, Brian Richardson, and Steve Wright shaped much of this text. Through extensive research and editing, Chris Cowan of the Council for Biblical Manhood and Womanhood strengthened several significant segments of the book. By grading mounds of student worksheets and research papers while this book underwent many drafts and edits, my Garrett Fellow Lilly Park carved out the extra time that I needed to complete this project.

The process of writing and editing the book began in the summer of 2008 at Java Brewing Company on Frankfort Avenue in Louisville. The text reached its completion six months later at the Starbucks

Café on Shelbyville Road in Fairmeade, Kentucky. The most mean-ingful encouragements throughout this process came not from edi-tors or agents or deans but from two jewels that God has lovingly set in the center of my life—my wife Rayann and our daughter Hannah. I could never deserve such great grace as I have been given through my wife and my daughter. And yet I rejoice each moment in their love, constantly reminded of how God has filled my life through them with immeasurable goodness and grace.

# Foreword
## Family Ministry and the Future of the Church

Over the last two years I have become aware that there is a genuine family ministry movement happening in the evangelical community, a movement involving churches of all sizes and denominations. At nearly every youth or children's conference, there are seminars dedicated to the subject of family ministry featuring multiple speakers presenting their perspectives on how it ought to be done. What is causing this groundswell of interest in family ministry? And why is this movement so significant?

First, family ministry is necessary and significant because families are under siege. They have been under siege since the beginning of time. When God declared in the third chapter of Genesis that the serpent would bruise the heel of the woman's offspring but that her offspring would crush the serpent's head, God invoked a declaration of war. From that point to this one, it has been the enemy's hellish strategy to undermine families. There is a bull's-eye on the back of every home, and the church must reorient itself to protect and to develop families.

Second, family ministry is necessary and significant because husbands and fathers have been marginalized. If Satan's strategy has been to undermine the home generally, his more specific strategy has been to marginalize husbands and fathers. In the garden of Eden, the serpent came to tempt the woman (Gen 3:1), undermining God's design for her husband to guide and to protect her. Yet, in the aftermath of the fall, God came looking for

Adam (3:9). Why? Because Adam was responsible for that family unit. He was responsible to guard his home. The contemporary church has made it too easy for husbands and fathers to follow Adam's example of neglecting their responsibilities at home. Dad is working too much, pursuing his own personal pleasures instead of sacrificially providing spiritual leadership for his family. Contrast this too-familiar pattern to God's ideal, expressed through the pen of the prophet Malachi: "He will turn the hearts of fathers to their children and the hearts of children to their fathers" (Mal 4:6). Any church failing to reach men and turn their hearts toward their families will be perpetually weak. A church that wants to pursue God's best must reorient itself to reach husbands and fathers and to hold them accountable for the most important job they will ever have.

Third, family ministry is necessary and significant because what we have been doing is ineffective. Today's churches offer more youth camps, conferences, Christian music, sophisticated technology, books, and trained leaders than ever before. Yet, for whatever reason, a significant number of children fail to make the transition from youth ministry to mature, Christian adulthood. The sort of ministry that will address this problem can't be found by adding one more church program found on the shelf of a Christian bookstore. Seminary classes cannot solve this problem. Not even this book can solve the problem. What is needed is a theological and structural reorientation spawning church cultures that draw families together instead of pulling them apart.

Fourth, family ministry is necessary and significant because the church is a family. I long to see a new climate sweep through our churches—a climate where families are drawn together, where dads are equipped to lead, where parents embrace the primary responsibility of discipling their children, where children's hearts are turned toward their mothers and fathers, where the hearts of mothers and fathers are turned toward their children, where the people of God make a place for single moms and shattered families and teenagers who come without parents. All of this is significant because, according to Scripture, the church is a family. Every believer in Jesus Christ has "received the Spirit of adoption" (Rom 8:15). God is the heavenly Father (Matt 6:9) who disciplines us like children (Heb 12:5–11). The church is the family of God, and family relationships represent a divinely ordained paradigm for God's church, which is why it is so important for our relationships in the family and in the church to reflect God's ideal. When congregations fail to conform to God's Word in every area, it becomes easy to let husbands and fathers off the hook, to embrace ministry models that do not hold parents accountable for the discipleship of their children, or to allow the church's many programs to fragment families instead of unifying them. When this happens, it is usually because the church has leaned too heavily on human pragmatism as opposed to a robust dependence on the sufficiency and authority of Scripture. It may be painful to realign the church's proclamation and practices. It may be hard work, and it may require repentance. But it is never wrong.

Fifth, family ministry is necessary and significant because families are waiting to be led. Right now in churches all over the country, families see the problems, and they are waiting for solutions. They are waiting to be led. Are you prepared to guide them? If you're ready to take the lead in these transitions, this book will serve as an invaluable resource to equip you with the knowledge you will need to guide families in your church toward a better way.

*Randy Stinson, Ph.D.*
Dean of the School of Leadership and Church Ministry
The Southern Baptist Theological Seminary

PART 1

# *Why Every Church Needs Family Ministry*
*by Timothy Paul Jones*

# CHAPTER 1

# *Confessions of a Well-Meaning Youth Minister*

"This is Wednesday night *youth group*. We don't *do* Bibles here."

After six years as a pastor, perhaps my life had grown too predictable. For reasons that weren't readily apparent at the time, God had moved me from the pastorate to youth ministry. It wasn't quite the move I anticipated as I completed degrees in ministry and biblical studies. Yet it was, without any doubt, God's direction. And I was confident that I would do well. I had, after all, been trained in the latest methods of Christian education and youth ministry during the studies that led to my master of divinity degree. So I began the process of searching for a student ministry position.

A few months later a mid-sized congregation near Tulsa, Oklahoma, called me as their youth minister. I moved from proclaiming the Scriptures from the pulpit each Sunday morning to routing hormonally charged couples out of closets during lock-ins, coming up with mathematical formulas for how many middle-schoolers it takes to consume a medium-sized pizza, and explaining to the maintenance committee how the moshing that resulted in a six-foot hole in the sheetrock really was congruent with the church's overall ministry strategy.

It was a promising position. The youth had their own activities, separate from the rest of the congregation, and the church budget provided funds to support these activities. The church was in the process of building an exclusive domain for the youth in an upper floor of the family life center so that neither youth nor adults disturbed one another. What's more, my predecessor in this position had attracted sixty or more students each Wednesday evening, and more than one hundred students each year for church camp. Attendance on Wednesday nights had dropped into the twenties after the previous minister's departure, but everyone in the congregation seemed certain that, as soon as they called a new youth minister, the numbers would race back to their previous peak.

They were wrong.

On my first Wednesday evening at the church, I received my first hint that this task might be more difficult than I'd imagined. After a couple of games, I gathered the students for some high-energy worship songs. Worship didn't seem to be part of what they expected, but I persisted anyway. At the end of the musical set, I leaned my guitar against an amplifier, lifted my Bible over my head, and asked, "OK, how many of you brought your Bibles?"

At first no one responded.

And that's when he said it.

A senior in high school, a five-year veteran of this particular youth group.

"This is Wednesday night *youth group*. We don't *do* Bibles here," he said. "And we don't come here to sing either. We're here to have fun."

In the silence that followed his statement, my first thought was simply, *Oh God, what am I going to do?*

## Doing My Best

That question would wend its way through my mind many more times in the upcoming months. Over the next few weeks, I persisted in my focus, and I discovered that this senior wasn't alone in his motivations for attending youth events. Numbers plunged into the low double digits. Parents complained to the pastor that their children weren't having enough fun. Church members who were unaware that the previous minister's weekly program consisted of an hour of games, horseplay, and occasional hazing, with a devotional tacked at the end, wondered why youth attendance on Wednesdays hadn't spiraled into the seventies and beyond.

What's worse, it wasn't only on Wednesdays that fewer youth were showing up. The previous youth minister provided pizza and games after church nearly every Sunday evening. Wanting to train students in spiritual disciplines, I plugged a small-group Bible study into that time slot, but only a couple of students were willing to engage in such an endeavor. Once the students discovered I didn't plan to sponsor such an event every Sunday, youth attendance plummeted on Sundays, too. The ones who *did* make an appearance on Sundays huddled together in a corner in the back of the worship center with a strong interest in note-passing and little interest in anything the pastor had to say.

I spent most of that first year torn between the conflicting expectations of the pastor, parents, students, and my own conscience. The pastor wanted greater numbers of youth and peace with the parents of these youth. The youth wanted a constant string of entertaining events. The parents wanted entertaining events too, but they also expected these activities, in some inexplicable way, to result in their children's spiritual maturity. From the perspective of these parents, I was the person hired for the tasks of discipling and entertaining their children.

For a while I remained passionate about my perceived responsibility to serve as the primary disciple-maker in these students' lives. Then, after a few months of frustration, I just wanted *out*. I tried to quit perhaps a half-dozen times during the first couple of years. I searched for other positions, but God persisted in interrupting every escape route. So I stuck it out, torn amid conflicting expectations that I could not seem to fulfill.

Near the end of my first year, I turned toward the heavens and raised a white flag of surrender. *Maybe,* I concluded, *I'm just not cut out for this ministry; but, God, until you move me, I will do my best to do it well. No matter what, I will work my hardest to do in this place whatever it is that you want me to do.*

And I did.

---

### What if Boredom Isn't Always Bad?

The founder of Young Life once commented, "It's a sin to bore a kid with the gospel." Is this statement true? How has this statement been applied in youth and children's ministries? How have these attitudes affected ministries to children and youth? After considering your own response to these questions, read what Mark DeVries has to say in response to the Young Life attitude: "It might be more of a sin to suggest to young people that the Christian life is always fun and never boring. Keeping teenagers from ever being bored in their faith can actually deprive them of opportunities to develop the discipline and perseverance needed to live the Christian life. It is precisely in those experiences that teenagers might describe as 'boring' that Christian character is often formed."[1] Do you agree with DeVries? Why or why not?

---

## Questioning the Assumptions

The student ministry did seem to improve during my second year. I established relationships in a nearby middle school and led many middle-schoolers to commit their lives to Christ. I trained a cluster of committed youth to serve as spiritual leaders. The youth group grew not in leaps and bounds but in a steady and sustained way. From the perspective of my congregation and other nearby churches, I seemed to be building a successful student ministry.

And still something wasn't quite right.

In the first place, so much of the student ministry seemed to center on my capacities to disciple the youth. At first this felt quite pleasant. After all, when students had needs, many of them came to me first, even before they went to their parents. Yet I quickly discovered that neither I nor my adult volunteers could sustain the spiritual lives of this many students.

---

1. M. DeVries, *Family-Based Youth Ministry* (Downers Grove, Ill.: InterVarsity, 1994).

There was also the fact that the fragmentation in so many students' families overwhelmed our efforts to effect transformation in the students' lives. And then there was the way the youth identified anything involving the adults of the church as "boring." My first response was to create youth-focused alternatives to every adult activity, but somehow this didn't draw the students to deeper commitment. In fact, it actually seemed to feed their immaturity.

Over time I began to see that the problems ran deeper than the spiritual immaturity of this particular group of youth. The difficulties ran even deeper than *my* immaturity—though, admittedly, that had been a factor in the first few months of my ministry. The problems had to do with how I and the church envisioned and defined successful student ministry.

That's when I began to ask some painful questions about student ministry that my training in youth ministry and Christian education had not equipped me to answer. *What if,* I wondered, *this separation between students and adults—something that I was trained to see as a solution—has actually been part of the problem? What if God never intended youth ministry staff members to become the primary sustainers of students' spiritual lives? What if something is profoundly wrong with the entire way the church has structured ministries to youth and children? What if the reason so many ministers are bordering on burnout is because our ministry models are fundamentally flawed?*

I didn't find answers to all these questions during my years in youth ministry. Some of the answers came later, after I was privileged to become the associate pastor and then the senior pastor in the same congregation where I first served as youth minister (a church that, to this day, remains the most wonderful congregation of believers I have ever served). And, truth be told, I'm still working toward complete answers to a couple of these questions. After several years of research and consultation with hundreds of pastors, churches, parents, youth, and children, however, I have made a good bit of progress. I hope my progress on this journey will help you walk the path on which God has placed you.

I must admit, though, that the first step on this journey sounds a little macabre: It entails learning how to murder a one-eared Mickey Mouse.

---

### What Causes Youth Ministers to Quit?

For many years youth ministers tended to remain only a year or two in the same congregation. In the twenty-first century, youth ministers are staying longer in their congregations. A 2002 survey of full-time youth ministers revealed an average tenure in each congregation of four years, seven months. The most frequent reasons given for leaving a church included inadequate salaries and conflicts with a senior pastor.[2]

---

## One-Eared Mice, Well-Meaning Ministers, and the Octopus without a Brain

In the late 1980s, one student minister depicted the relationship between his ministry and the rest of his congregation as a "one-eared Mickey Mouse."[3] The head of the cartoon mouse represented the church as a whole, and the ear represented youth ministry. His point was simply this: Like the ear of the renowned rodent on Walt Disney's drawing board, his ministry was barely connected to the rest of the body. Although the student ministry and the larger congregation were technically linked, the two operated on separate tracks, with each one pursuing its own purposes and passions.

His church wasn't alone, and it still isn't.

Somehow in the past century this approach has prevailed in many churches as the dominant model for student ministry. The model has become so popular that, in many instances, it has turned into the predominant paradigm not only for youth ministry but also for preschool, children's, and singles ministries. The one-eared Mickey Mouse has metamorphosed into a multi-eared mutant—or, to use another youth leader's memorable image, something like "an octopus without a brain, a collection of arms

2. J. Grenz, "Factors Influencing Vocational Changes among Youth Ministers," *Journal of Youth Ministry* (2002): 73–88.

3. C. Clark, "From Fragmentation to Integration":www.forministry.com/vsItemDisplay .dsp&objectID=E72737BD-864C-4E53-A419FFCE44955BCF&method=display&templat eID=C3435351-D45C-4B52-867A3F794D1CD85C.

acting independently with no central processing unit coordinating their actions."[4]

As this ministry model has developed, here's what has tended to happen: *Parents are not perceived as having the primary responsibility for the spiritual growth of their offspring.* Age-specific ministers in the church have increasingly embraced the primary responsibility for discipling students and children. Children and youth experience their activities and worship in virtual isolation from the remainder of the church, and parents need only drop off their progeny at the appropriate times.

In 2006, Richard Ross, a professor at Southwestern Baptist Theological Seminary, predicted that at some point in the future churches would begin to

> build buildings to support segregation—and they will do it with *excellence.* They will not build for racial segregation, but to support age segregation. . . . Both the natural appeal of such buildings and the programming centered there will guarantee [that] teenagers will only experience church life with people almost precisely their own age. Adults will find no ways to bless children, much less even see them. Young people will be cut off from the richness of almost all adult relationships. And, most importantly, they will not see members of their own families until it is time to meet at their cars to go home.[5]

On only one point do I disagree with Ross's assessment: What he has described is not merely the theoretical church of the future but the actual, present predicament of many current congregations.

When this programmatic model dominates a church's ministries, students' and children's ministers may see parents in passing, but they do little to transform parents' relationships with their offspring. (After all, don't Sunday school, children's church, and youth group provide the principal contexts for the disciple-

---

4. C. Clark, *The Youth Worker's Handbook to Family Ministry* (Grand Rapids, Mich.: Zondervan, 1997), 24.

5. R. Ross, "What Will Church Be Like in Ten Years?" Presentation to the NNYM Executive Council, 2006: www.ymnetwork.org/future_of_YM/Churches_Future-Ross.doc.

ship of the church's students?) "Success" is defined in terms of high-energy events that students experience in virtual isolation from other generations. Such youth and children's ministries seem to expect students to become integrated with their families at home even as they model the dis-integration of their families at church.

So why has this model survived so long?

It seems to me that in many congregations a single false assumption has maintained the mutant mouse's vigor long after it should have become clear that his nose was twitching in the wrong direction. The false assumption is simply this: *Parents are not the primary persons responsible for their children's Christian formation.* The people perceived as being primarily responsible for children's spiritual development are specialized leaders of age-focused ministries. Despite the popularity of this model, here's what I wish to suggest: *This model is not biblical, and the results of this approach have not consistently reflected God's intentions for His people.*

Please don't misread my point: I am *not* claiming that age-focused ministers have unbiblical intentions. As an associate pastor, senior pastor, and now as a professor, I've worked with hundreds of ministers and would-be ministers to children and youth. As I reflect on my conversations with these men and women, I can say with complete confidence that, with few exceptions, each of them possesses a sincere and passionate desire to devise ministries that conform completely to God's Word.

I am also *not* blaming the difficulties that I've described on youth ministry. What I have described is *not* a problem with youth ministry! It is an issue that involves the assumptions and practices of the entire congregation. Furthermore, I am *not* suggesting that every church with a youth or children's minister is necessarily pursuing the maladapted model of ministry I describe in this chapter.

Here is what I *am* suggesting: The ministry models that many ministers have studied in seminaries and inherited in local churches are fundamentally flawed. As a result, well-intended ministers have attempted to pursue tasks in the sole context of the church that God designed to occur first and foremost in another context.

That other context is the *family*.

---

### Structures, Schedules, and Age Segregation

Sketch your church's organizational structure. Then summarize each of your church's weekly activities. Draw lines that connect the weekly activities to elements of the organizational structure. Do your church's programs and structures contribute more to *coordination* or to *separation* within each family in your church? How could your church do a better job of bringing families together?

CHAPTER 2

# *The Task Too Significant to Hire Someone Else to Do*

There are some tasks so significant that you're better off doing them yourself.

Taking your spouse on a date, for example.

Think of it this way: Suppose I called my wife this afternoon and announced, "Honey, guess what? Remember how you asked about a date tonight? Well, I hired a *professional dater* to take you to dinner and a movie. Yes, that's right, dear: A professional! He's much better at dating than me—plus, since I'll be at home watching *Star Wars*, we won't need a babysitter. Have a great time!"

Now, if such an evening seemed even *remotely* interesting to my wife, let's just say that she and I have more problems than any date—professional or otherwise—can possibly fix! In fact, if I seriously suggested such an evening, I suspect that many cold nights would pass before my wife requested a date with me again. Why? Because some tasks are too significant to be surrendered to professionals. Other people may remind you to perform such tasks; others may even equip you to perform them better. But no other person possesses the proper qualifications to carry them out.

It is also that way when it comes to the discipleship of our children.

The church may remind me to disciple our daughter. Ministers, elders, or deacons might even equip Rayann and me to disciple Hannah more effectively. Yet the task of training our

daughter to follow Jesus Christ is too significant to be surrendered wholly to professionals. No one else possesses the proper
qualifications to embrace this primary responsibility because no
one else can lay claim to the title of Hannah's father or mother.

Not everyone seems to feel this way, though. I suggest (based
not only on my own experiences but also on a good bit of research
in the area[1]) that most Christian parents are perfectly willing
to let their church provide all their children's religious instruction. In some cases, this is because parents assume that the spiritual maturity of their children is primarily the responsibility of
professional ministers in their churches. In other instances, it
seems that parents may intend to develop their children spiritually, but they simply do not know how to engage personally in
the discipleship of their children.

To gain a practical glimpse of what I'm talking about, try
this experiment: Scan as many mission statements from church-
based youth or children's ministries as you can possibly find. In
most mission statements, what you find are firm commitments
to evangelize, equip, and entertain children or youth—all within
the context of age-focused and age-segmented ministries. According to one such statement from a youth group's Web site,
student ministry exists to *"reproduce* disciples for Christ out
of unbelieving youth, *rebuild* their spiritual life, increase their
faith to *reverence* God through *relationships*, and care for others through *restoration*."[2] Another ministry plans "to evangelize, equip, and engage as many middle school and high school
students for Jesus Christ as possible" and "to teach, mature, and
train those who are seeking to become committed followers."[3]
On another Web site a youth pastor declares that his personal
mission is "to mobilize an army of youth who intimately love
Jesus and want to share him with others."[4]

1. See,e.g.,Barna Research Group,"Parents Accept Responsibility for Their Child's Spiritual Development but Struggle with Effectiveness": www.barna.org/FlexPage.aspx?Page=
BarnaUpdate&BarnaUpdateID=138.

2. FCC Youth Ministry: www.nnym.net/sites/fccyouth.

3. Variations of this mission statement may be found in many student ministries
including, e.g., www.parksidechurch.com/site/c.iqLRIUOCKtF/b.1467761/k.C816/Youth
.htm and www.bonnersferryfmc.com/youth.htm.

4. R. Nielsen: www.youthpastor.com/lessons/index.cfm/Philosophy-Youth_Ministry_
Philosophy_Strategy_and_Program_61.htm.

What you will typically never find in these mission statements is *any* clear expression of how the student ministry plans to partner with parents to disciple children. In fact, I read more than a hundred mission statements and strategies on student-ministry Web sites before I found one that even *mentioned* the role of parents in their children's lives; and that was in a single sentence fragment, tacked near the statement's final paragraph. What does this pattern suggest about these congregations' expectations when it comes to the discipleship of children and youth?

---

**Church Mission Statements and Parental Responsibilities**
Look at some mission statements from the ministries in your church. Do these statements rightly reflect the responsibility of parents to disciple their children? In what ways could you change these statements to reflect this responsibility?

---

## *Turning the Hearts of Children to Their Fathers*

Such mission statements stand in stark contrast to the explicit expectations of Holy Scripture. When God chose Abraham to father a mighty nation, part of God's purpose for the father of the Hebrews was that he would "command his children and his house after him to keep the way of the LORD" (Gen 18:19). Later, when Moses received the law of God, he passed on precise instructions regarding how the people should embed the precepts in their hearts:

> These words that I am giving you today are to be in your heart. Repeat them to your children. Talk about them when you sit in your house and when you walk along the road, when you lie down and when you get up. . . . Be careful not to forget the LORD. (Deut 6:6–7,12; see also Exod 12:25–28; Deut 11:1–12)

To this very day, Orthodox Jews recite these words every morning and every evening, reminding themselves of God's plan for the preservation of their people. Even in the songs of Israel, the primary responsibility for children's spiritual formation fell to parents. A songwriter named Asaph put it this way:

I will declare wise sayings . . . that our fathers have passed down to us. We must not hide them from their children, but must tell a future generation the praises of the LORD, . . . so that a future generation—children yet to be born—might know. They were to rise and tell their children so that they might put their confidence in God. (Ps 78:2–4,6–7)

In the prologue to his proverbs, one of Israel's ancient sages reminded youth to learn divine wisdom in the context of their homes: "Listen, my son, to your father's instruction, and don't reject your mother's teaching" (Prov 1:8).

In the centuries after the events described in the Old Testament, synagogues emerged as dedicated contexts for prayer and study of the Hebrew Scriptures. Still, the Jewish home remained the primary locus of children's spiritual training.[5] At least until the mid-first century AD, education was perceived primarily as the Jewish father's responsibility,[6] and Jewish teachers seem to have considered a child's presence in synagogue schools to be optional.[7] Even when children *did* attend synagogue schools, the religious leaders still expected each Jewish home to be "viewed, much like the tabernacle, as a private sanctuary for religious observances, including the worship of God, . . . the instruction in the Torah, . . . and meeting needs found in the community."[8]

Similar expectations persisted through the New Testament era, especially in the epistles of Paul. From Paul's perspective, delegating the discipleship of one's child to a professional minister does not appear to have been a legitimate possibility. The

---

5. See, e.g., K. Lawson, "Historical Foundations of Christian Education," in *Introducing Christian Education,* ed. M. Anthony (Grand Rapids, Mich.: Baker, 2001), 18. The community gatherings in the synagogue seem to have been geared toward adults; parents were, in turn, expected to express precepts to their children in ways that the children could comprehend.

6. O. M. Bakke, *When Children Became People,* trans. B. McNeil (Philadelphia, Penn.: Fortress, 2005), 176.

7. For exploration of the function of synagogue schools, see M. Anthony, ed., "Synagogue Schools," in *Evangelical Dictionary of Christian Education* (Grand Rapids, Mich.: Baker, 2001); N. Drazin, *History of Jewish Education from 515 BCE to 220 CE* (New York: Arno, 1979), 46; J. Reed and R. Prevost, *A History of Christian Education* (Nashville, Tenn.: B&H, 1998), 49; W. A. Strange, *Children in the Early Church: Children in the Ancient World, the New Testament and the Early Church* (Carlisle, Cumbria, UK: Paternoster, 1996), 13.

8. M. Anthony and W. Benson, *Exploring the History and Philosophy of Christian Education* (Grand Rapids, Mich.: Kregel, 2003), 27.

apostle assumed that believing fathers would train their children through encouragement and comfort, urging them to live lives "worthy of God" (1 Thess 2:11–12).[9] In his letters to Christians in Asia Minor, he specifically commanded fathers to bring up their offspring "in the training and instruction of the Lord" without frustrating or discouraging them (Eph 6:4; Col 3:21).

Perhaps most important of all, a primary evidence of the in-breaking of God's reign—predicted by the prophet Malachi, proclaimed by John the Baptist, and consummated through the presence of Jesus Christ—was that, in believing households, the hearts of children would be turned toward their fathers, and the hearts of fathers would be turned toward their children (Mal. 4:6; Luke 1:17). When evangelism, worship, and discipleship for children and youth occur in isolation from, and, at times, with disdain for, their adult counterparts, it is difficult to see how the hearts of parents and children can consistently be turned toward one another.

As I examine the expectations of Scripture, I find woven throughout its pages that neither the temple nor the synagogue nor professional ministers bore the first responsibility for training children to be followers of God. The home provided a primary context for discipleship, and parents were expected to serve as primary disciple-makers.

## Family Discipleship in the History of the Church

The expectation of family discipleship didn't end with the New Testament era. Two early Christian documents, *Didache* and *Letter of Barnabas,* provide summaries of Christian practices that date to the first and second centuries AD. Both of these writings include an identical command for parents, a command evidently oft-repeated in the early churches: "You shall train [your son and your daughter] in the fear of God from their youth up."[10]

A second-century church leader named Polycarp specifically held husbands responsible to partner with their wives "to

9. In 1 Thess 2:11–12, Paul seems to have *assumed* the believing father's involvement in his children's lives, so much so that he called on the example of a believing father to bolster his defense of his own apostleship.

10. *Didache* 4:9; *Epistle of Barnabas* 19.5.

train their children in the fear of God."[11] Another leader in the early church, Clement of Rome, urged parents to embrace the privilege of sharing with their children "the instruction that is in Christ."[12] The church father John Chrysostom described the process of parenthood in terms of training children to be "athletes for Christ."[13] And how were parents to coach their children toward godliness? According to Chrysostom:

> To each of you fathers and mothers, I speak: Just as we see artists fashioning their paintings and statues with great precision, so we must care for these wondrous statues of ours. Painters, once they have set the canvas on the easel, paint on it day by day to accomplish their purpose. Sculptors, too, working in marble, proceed in a similar manner; they remove what is unhelpful and add what is lacking. You should proceed in the same way. Like the creators of statues, give all your leisure time to fashioning these wondrous statues of God. As you remove what is unhelpful and add what is lacking, inspect them day by day, to see with which good qualities nature has supplied them so that you can increase these qualities, and to see which faults so that you can eradicate them.[14]

---

### How to Do Great Things for God

As a pastor, I make this statement to my church: "What you do for God beyond your home will not typically be greater than what you practice with God within your home."[15] Do you agree with this statement? Why or why not?

---

11. Polycarp of Smyrna, *To the Philippians*, 4:2.

12. Clement of Rome, *First Epistle*, 21:6-8.

13. John Chrysostom, *De Inani*, 19; 39; 63; 90. M. Anthony suggests that "children were not viewed as an educational priority" in the church's early centuries—a statement that, from my perspective, historical evidences do not substantiate ("Childhood Education," in Anthony, *Introducing Christian Education*, 206). Education of children in age-focused groupings was not common, the content presented in church contexts was not focused on the needs of children per se, and the Christian home provided the primary context for Christian education of children. However, the Christian education of children *was* an extremely high priority for the early churches, evidenced by the high expectations placed on parents not only in *Didache, Epistle of Barnabas*, and *Shepherd of Hermas* but also in the later homilies of John Chrysostom.

14. John Chrysostom, *De Inani*, 22.

15. Quoted in G. Wishall, "SBTS adds noted author, pastor to School of Leadership faculty," *Towers*: Retrieved from www.towersonline.net/story.php?grp=towers&id=284.

## The Task Too Significant for Anyone Else to Do

Somehow, these expectations have shifted over the centuries, though. Especially in the past couple of centuries, church programs have usurped a responsibility that Scripture and church history place first and foremost at the feet of parents.

At this point it is crucial for us to recognize what is *not* new about our present practices. Organizing church members according to their ages or their needs is *not* new. In churches of the third century AD (probably even earlier) all the generations worshiped together, but men, women, and young people sat separately.[16] In the early fifth century AD, Augustine of Hippo taught catechetical classes that intermingled children with farmers, city dwellers, illiterate folk, professional grammarians, and public speakers.[17] More than a millennium later, Jonathan Edwards gathered groups of young people for age-organized Bible studies. In December 1743, Jonathan Edwards wrote these words to a personal acquaintance:

> At the conclusion of the public exercise on the Sabbath, I appointed the children that were under sixteen years of age to go from the meetinghouse to a neighbor house, that I there might further enforce what they had heard in public, and might give in some counsels proper for their age.[18]

---

16. *Didascalia Apostolorum* 12: "Let the men sit in another part of the house, toward the east. . . . If anyone be found sitting out of his place, let the deacon who is within reprove him and make him to rise up and sit in a place that is appropriate for him. . . . Let the children stand on one side, or let their fathers and mothers take them to them; and let them stand up. Let the young girls also sit apart; but if there be no room, let them stand up behind the women. Let the young women who are married and have children stand apart, and the aged women and widows sit apart. . . . Let the deacon also see that no one whispers, or falls asleep, or laughs, or makes gestures. For so it should be, that with decency and decorum they watch in the Church, with ears attentive to the word of the Lord."

17. "Sed illud plane non praetereundum est, ut si ad te quisquam catechizandus venerit liberalibus doctrinis excultus, qui iam decreverit esse christianus. . . . Sunt item quidam de scholis usitatissimis grammaticorum oratorumque venientes. . . . Iam vero si usitata et parvulis congruentia saepe repetere fastidimus: congruamus eis per fraternum, paternum, maternumque amorem, et copulatis cordi eorum etiam nobis nova videbuntur" (Augustine of Hippo, *De Catechizandis Rubidis Liber Unus,* 8, 9, 12: www.augustinus .it/latino/catechesi_cristiana/index.htm.)

18. J. Edwards, "Letter to the Reverend Thomas Prince of Boston," December 12, 1743: www.nhinet.org/ccs/docs/awaken.htm.

Later in the eighteenth century, Robert Raikes taught and evangelized clusters of street children in early Sunday schools.[19]

The failure of some Christian parents to disciple their children is also *not* new. In one popular Christian writing from the mid-second-century AD, a divine messenger tells the protagonist that "the Lord is angry" with him because he's fallen short in the spiritual formation of his children.[20] In the eighteenth century, Jonathan Edwards found it necessary to admonish his congregation with these words:

> Every Christian family ought to be as it were a little church, consecrated to Christ, and wholly influenced and governed by His rules. And family education and order are some of the chief means of grace. If these fail, all other means are likely to prove ineffectual.[21]

If neither age-organized ministries nor failures to fulfill parental responsibilities are recent phenomena, what *is* new? What is relatively new is the assumption that specialized church ministries can or should become the main means by which Christian children mature in their faith. The idea that *any* age-focused ministry possesses the capacity or principal responsibility to lead students toward spiritual maturity represents a radical departure not only from the teachings of Scripture but also from centuries of Christian expectations and practice. Yet that seems to be precisely the perspective of many contemporary Christian parents and churches. The discipleship of children is perceived to be the task of the church's programs, not of the children's parents.

## *"Spiritual Drop-Off Service"?*

In a 2003 survey, for example, 85 percent of Christian parents admitted that they were responsible for their child's spiritual development. Yet, even as these parents outwardly admitted this responsibility, the vast majority were not personally engag-

---

19. R. Lynn and E. Wright, *The Big Little School* (Birmingham, Ala.: Religious Education, 1971), 55–57.

20. *Shepherd of Hermas* 1:3:1; 2:2:2.

21. J. Edwards, "A Farewell Sermon": www.sermonaudio.com/sermoninfo.asp?SID=370611425.

ing in *any* activities that might guide their children to spiritual maturity, except for the fact that two-thirds of these parents did regularly take their children to church.

With few exceptions these parents had no plans for their children's spiritual training, had never personally engaged in any activity that might develop their children spiritually, and had experienced no training and no accountability in their churches for such a task. "Most parents," the pollsters concluded, "proclaim that the spiritual nurturing of their children is their job, but [they] are very happy to let their church shape the child's faith."[22] Parents believed they were fulfilling their responsibility for their child's spiritual formation simply by involving them in church programs.

Why have Christian parents failed to treat their children's spiritual development as their personal priority? Well, why should they, when age-focused ministers have already accepted that responsibility? Why should a parent prioritize spiritual formation when, according to the student minister's own purpose statement, this paid professional already has plans in place "to mobilize an army of youth who intimately love Jesus"? Why should parents plan to disciple their children, when the church has already promised "to teach, mature, and train" these children, all within the context of children's and student ministries?

From the perspective of too many parents, schoolteachers are responsible to grow their children's minds, coaches are employed to train their bodies, and specialized ministers at church ought to develop their souls. When it comes to schooling and coaching, these perspectives may or may not be particularly problematic. When it comes to Christian formation, however, this perspective faces a single critical snag: God specifically calls believing parents to the task of training their children in the Christian faith. This is one task that, from the perspective of Scripture, parents simply cannot hire someone else to do.

---

22. Barna Research Group, "Parents Accept Responsibility" (see chap. 2, n. 6).

Yet churches and parents alike continue to "view student ministry . . . as a spiritual drop-off service best left to the professionals."[23] As Mike Yaconelli has noted,

> Every week local churches [look] for someone—anyone—to work with their youth. . . . These churches are desperate to find someone who will "do something" with their kids. Punch on to the job listings on the Youth Specialties Web site: . . . Hundreds of churches are eager to find someone who will form their children in the Christian faith. What's happened? Why are we so eager to hand the spiritual development of our young people to the first person we find who can locate the New Testament and needs a little part-time work?[24]

Indeed, what *has* happened? Why do so many contemporary Christians expect specialized student ministries to accomplish what Scripture has clearly commanded parents to do? And what can churches do to equip these parents to pursue the task that God has ordained for them?

In recent years, what churches can do has been encapsulated in two words: *Family ministry*. Here's the difficulty, though: Although there's widespread agreement that churches *ought* to do family ministry, there's little agreement regarding *what* family ministry looks like. And there is even less agreement when it comes to the question of *how* to implement a family ministry.

To understand why family ministry is needed and how such a ministry might be implemented, let's first develop a deeper understanding of our present predicament. Specifically, let's take a quick trip through the past two centuries, to explore the birth of the American teenager and the beginnings of age-segregated ministry. After surveying the cultural and sociological histories behind us, perhaps we will be able to see more clearly the problems and the possibilities before us.

23. S. Wright with C. Graves, *reThink* (Raleigh, N.C.: InQuest, 2007), 47.
24. M. Yaconelli, "Youth Ministry: A Contemplative Approach," *Christian Century* (April 21, 1999): 450.

## The Barna Group's Research into Parental Responsibility for Children's Spiritual Formation

"Close to nine out of ten parents of children under age 13 (85%) believe they have the primary responsibility for teaching their children about religious beliefs and spiritual matters. . . . Related research, however, revealed that a majority of parents do not spend any time during a typical week discussing religious matters or studying religious materials with their children. . . . About two out of three parents of children 12 or younger attend religious services at least once a month and generally take their children with them. . . . The survey data indicate that parents generally rely upon their church to do all of the religious training their children will receive. Parents are not so much unwilling to provide more substantive training to their children as they are ill-equipped to do such work. . . . Only one out of every five parents of children under 13 (19%) has ever been personally contacted or spoken to by a church leader to discuss the parents' involvement in the spiritual life and development of their youngsters."[25]

---

25. Barna Research Group, "Parents Accept Responsibility."

CHAPTER 3

# *Historical Contexts for Family Ministry*

In the twentieth century, a novel phenomenon grew to predominance in Western culture. The title of this cultural invention?

The teenager.

Believe it or not, the very word *teenager* wasn't coined until 1941, and the word didn't appear in English dictionaries until the 1950s![1] Of course, people in every historical epoch have endured a transition from childhood to adulthood. So, in one sense, the years of youthful transition are as ancient as Cain and Abel. And, to the best of my knowledge, no one in *any* generation has figured out how to skip the years between the twelfth and the twentieth birthdays—though, if anyone ever places such a plan on the market, I predict that it will be a big seller. Complaints about youth are also ancient. In the fifth century BC, the philosopher Socrates registered this grievance regarding the adolescents in Athens: "Youth . . . have bad manners, contempt for authority; they . . . love chatter in place of exercise."[2]

The fact of adolescence is ancient, but the function of the adolescent years took on a new face in the second half of twentieth century. What emerged for the first time during these de-

---

1. D. West, *The Death of the Grown-Up* (New York: St. Martin's, 2007), chapter 1.
2. Quoted in D. Walsh and N. Bennett, *Why Do They Act That Way?* (New York: Free Press, 2005), 1.

cades was a distinct adolescent culture differing radically from the culture of parents and other adults.[3] The teenage years shifted from an intermediary life-stage with the goal of adulthood to a distinct social and cultural structure that resisted movement toward adulthood. This created a rupture based not on divergent cultural backgrounds but on the conflicting values of successive generations. Never before had a cleft of quite this sort occurred. Here's how journalist Walter Kirn summarized this cultural shift:

> Of all the great postwar inventions—television, rock-n-roll, the Internet—the greatest and most influential is, perhaps, the American teenager. . . . While the country has always had adolescents, . . . it was only in the past 50 or 60 years that it had tens of millions of semi-grownups living in a developmental buffer zone somewhere between childish innocence and adult experience. . . . Early twentieth-century adolescents were farmers, apprentices, students and soldiers—perhaps even wives and husbands—but not teenagers. Spawned by a mix of prosperity and politics, teenagers are a modern luxury good.[4]

The roots of this "modern luxury good" are too complex to be explored completely in the present context. A few factors in this cultural transition are, however, crucial when it comes to understanding how to design and implement family ministries in the local church.

The rise of the teenager can be traced in part to the influence of the Industrial Revolution, to a psychologist named G. Stanley Hall, and to the popularity of the public high school in the economic upsurge that followed the Second World War. Let's look briefly at key factors in the history of adolescence and at how this development has impacted the church.

---

3. J. Kett, *Rites of Passage: Adolescence in America 1790 to the Present* (New York: Basic, 1977), 36.

4. W. Kirn, "Will Teenagers Disappear?" *Time* (February 21, 2000): Retrieved January 2, 2006, from www.time.com.

---

### Will Teenagers Disappear?

Walter Kirn suggests that the social phenomenon known as the "teenager" will cease to exist by the year 2020. "Teenagers, as classically defined, are already dying out, or at least changing into something different. The buffer zone they once inhabited is being squeezed out of existence for two reasons: children are growing up faster than ever before, and adults are growing up more slowly. . . . What will a world without teenagers look like? Like the adult world does now. Adolescents will feel the same pressures as their parents do: to succeed financially, to maintain their health, to stay on society's good side. What's more, adolescents will field these pressures using their elders' traditional techniques: spending money, taking medication, contracting for professional advice. The carefree years will become the prudent years, and the prudent years will continue throughout life. That's how it used to be, in the 19th century, and that's how it will be again in the 21st. The age of James Dean, the Ford Mustang and making out will seem, in retrospect, like what it was: a summer vacation from larger human history." Is Kirn correct? If so, how should churches respond to this cultural shift? If not, what do you suppose that adolescence will look like in the year 2020?

---

## *The Invention of Adolescence*

With the dawning of Westward Expansion in the late eighteenth century, church and community membership gave way to land ownership as essential elements of the American economy.[5] One upshot of this societal shift was, in the words of historian Stephen Keillor, a "patriarchal rebellion," a generation of pioneer men whose focus moved from their families and communities to saloons, shooting matches, and "long hunts."[6] In the nineteenth century, the Industrial Revolution introduced a parallel fracturing of family structures in areas far removed from the American frontier. Prior to the Industrial Revolution, children of every age had tended to work in their homes alongside family members from multiple generations.[7] As the Industrial

5. S. Keillor, *This Rebellious House* (Downers Grove, Ill.: InterVarsity, 1996), 109.
6. Ibid., 105–15.
7. J. Demos, *Past, Present and Personal: The Family and the Life Course in American History* (New York: Oxford University, 1986), 97. Between 1890 and 1990, the percentage of American juveniles working alongside their families in agrarian settings shifted from

Revolution reshaped Western culture, the primary locus of labor moved from farms to factories. Family members found themselves working in isolation from one another and often struggling simply to survive.

Equal education for all people became increasingly perceived as the panacea for society's problems. "Education, if equably diffused, will draw property after it by the strongest of all attractions," social reformer Horace Mann contended in 1848. "Education, beyond all other devices of human origin, is the great equalizer of the conditions of men—the balance-wheel of the social machinery."[8] Four years later Horace Mann and the governor of Massachusetts successfully pressed for the Prussian practice of compulsory school attendance in their state.[9]

In 1875, the Supreme Court laid the legal foundations for Horace Mann's "equably diffused" compulsory education at the high school level, when justices sanctioned the use of tax dollars to maintain free secondary schools for all citizens.[10] Public schools in which students were segregated according to grade levels gradually came to represent an American ideal. As increasing numbers of children and adolescents attended these schools, organizations such as the Young People's Society for Christian Endeavor emerged to provide opportunities for Christian youth to socialize and to learn together.[11]

The challenges of the Industrial Revolution and the campaign for equal education laid the foundations for the public

70 percent to less than 5 percent (T. Campolo, *Growing Up in America* [Grand Rapids, Mich.: Zondervan, 1989]).

8. H. Mann, "Report for 1848: The Capacity of the Common-School System to Improve the Pecuniary Condition, and Elevate the Intellectual, Moral, and Religious Character, of the Commonwealth," in *Annual Reports on Education* (Boston: Horace Fuller, 1868), 669.

9. To understand the effects of the Prussian model of compulsory schooling on the American educational system, see M. Rothbard, "Education: Free and Compulsory": www.mises.org/story/2226#11.

10. M. Cannister, "Youth Ministry's Historical Context," in *Starting Right: Thinking Theologically about Youth Ministry,* ed. K. Dean, et al. (Grand Rapids, Mich.: Zondervan,, 2001), 82; W. Reese, *The Origins of the American High School* (New Haven, Conn.: Yale University, 1999), 78; but cf. B. Burrell and R. Eckelberry, "The High School Question Before the Courts in the Post-Civil War Period," *The School Review* 42 (April 1934): 255–65.

11. Interestingly, even in the early 1900s, some Christian leaders expressed concern that these programs would "divide the church on the basis of age" (F. Erb, *The Development of the Young People's Movement* [Chicago: University of Chicago, 1917], 59).

high school. Yet it was psychologist G. Stanley Hall who most strongly influenced the educational structure of this new institution as well as public perceptions of adolescence. In 1904, Hall drew from Jean-Baptiste Lamarck's evolutionary theory to devise a map of human development and concluded that adolescence reflected an early, turbulent stage of human evolution. Adolescence "comes from and harks back to a remoter past," Hall claimed. "Development is . . . suggestive of some ancient period of storm and stress when old moorings were broken."[12] Because adolescence echoes a primeval shattering of "old moorings," social structures should, according to Hall, allow adolescents to "wander far and long enough to find the best habitat."[13] In the decades that followed Hall's research, the halls of the American high school became the primary context for the wandering that Hall prescribed.

The Great Depression strengthened the position of the high school in American culture. To increase the number of jobs available to adults, government agencies imposed new truancy laws and enforced existing school-attendance statutes,[14] forcing adolescents out of the workplace and into schools. As adolescents increasingly clustered together in public schools, separated from adults, Hall's perspective on adolescence "became the basis of the social definition of an entire age group."[15]

Throughout the twentieth century the content of the public education that these adolescents received grew increasingly secular. It was progressivist philosopher John Dewey who helped shape this tendency toward secularized education in American public schools. Like the seventeenth-century educator Jan Amos Comenius, John Dewey envisioned a universal system of education. Yet Dewey contended that this educational system ought

---

12. G .S. Hall, *Youth: Its Education, Regimen, and Hygiene*. Retrieved February 26, 2007, from www.gutenberg.org/dirs/etext05/8yuth10.txt. Hall's contentions regarding the stormy and stressful nature—the *Sturm und Drang*—of adolescence have been repeatedly called into question, most notably in the work of Daniel Offer. See, e.g., D. Offer, "The Mystery of Adolescence," *Adolescent Psychiatry* 14 (1987), 7–27.

13. Hall, *Youth*.

14. G. Palladino, *Teenagers: An American History* (New York: Basic, 1996), 12–15; Krug 1964, 168–200.

15. J. Kett, *Rites of Passage*, 215.

to adhere to a secularized "common faith,"[16] gutted of the God-centered framework that had been so essential to Comenius' vision.[17] Jan Amos Comenius had mandated that an inscription over the seventh classroom door must declare to all, "Let no one enter who is irreligious."[18] If John Dewey had envisaged an analogous portal, his would have declared something closer to, "Abandon any supernatural beliefs at the door."

By the late 1940s and 1950s, the widespread availability of secondary public education had coupled with the euphoria of postwar economic recovery to birth a new American ideal. This new ideal included the deep-seated supposition that, in the most respectable families, youth should be exempted from any responsibility to assist their families through meaningful labor.[19]

Perhaps most important, the youth of this era became the first generation in American history that consistently received enough spending money to impact the economy in significant ways. A 1958 article in *Billboard* magazine noted:

> Today's nine-to-fourteen-year-old group is the first generation with enough money given to them by their parents to buy records in sufficient quantities to influence the market. In my youth if I asked my father for forty-five cents to buy a record, he'd have thought seriously about having me committed.[20]

Partly because of this newfound spending power, the rising breed of adolescents also became the objects of another cultural

---

16. J. Dewey, *A Common Faith: Based on the Terry Lectures Delivered at Yale University* (New Haven, Conn.:Yale University Press, 1934), 1–3, 86, 87.

17. For the centeredness of Comenius's vision in religious motivations, see, e.g., the editor's introduction to J. Comenius, *School of Infancy* (Whitefish, Mont.: Kessinger, 2003), 9.

18. J. Comenius, *The Great Didactic of John Amos Comenius,* ed. M. Keatinge (London, UK: Adam and Charles Black, 1896), 146–47. Religious faith undergirds every aspect of the educational experience for Comenius: "In arithmetic the sacred and mystic numbers that occur in the Scriptures should be studied; also sacred architecture. . . . History should be studied, and in particular the history of the Church, for whose sake the world exists. . . . The accessory study is Hebrew, which must be studied in such a way that before the end of the year the pupil shall be able to read and understand the original text of the Scriptures."

19. S. Coontz, *The Way We Never Were* (New York: Basic Books, 1992), 13–14.

20. D. Halper, *Invisible Stars: A Social History of Women in American Broadcasting* (Armunk, New York: M. E. Sharpe, 2001), 179.

innovation: age-focused marketing. Eventually, not only teenagers but also children became targets of tightly niched marketing campaigns.

In the closing decades of the twentieth century, what had once seemed like a generational gap grew into a gaping chasm. Yet it wasn't primarily a movement of youth away from adults. It was adults, especially fathers, who gradually disappeared from children's spheres of existence, throwing themselves into their own pursuits of leisure and labor.[21] In an effort to retain their children's allegiance, parents pampered their children with more and more possessions. Adolescence became a time of maximal indulgence coupled with minimal responsibilities and minimal supervision. And thus parents, marketers, and adolescents unwittingly cooperated to create a youth culture that differed radically from the culture of their parents.

## *Living in a Tribe Apart*

Adolescents became—in the words of journalist Patricia Hersch—"a tribe apart."[22] By the close of the twentieth century, the typical American parent spent fewer than fifteen minutes each week in significant dialogue with his or her child. The percentage of parents highly or moderately involved in their children's lives declined from 75 percent in elementary school to 50 percent among middle schoolers.[23] Seventy-five percent of teenagers reported that they had *never* experienced a meaningful conversation with their fathers.[24] "A clear picture of adolescents, of even our own children, eludes us," Patricia Hersch observed, "not necessarily because they are rebelling, or avoiding or evading us. *It is because we aren't there.* Not just parents, but any adults. American society has left its children behind."[25]

---

21. Language alludes to G. Bredfeldt, *Ministry through the Lifespan,* self-published CD-ROM.

22. Hersch, *A Tribe Apart.* See also Keillor, *This Rebellious House,* 246–81. Cf. M. Mead, *Culture and Commitment: A Study of the Generation Gap* (Garden City, N.Y.: Doubleday, 1970), 30–35; but note that Margaret Mead's research was highly subjective and flawed in significant ways.

23. Cited in DeVries, *Family-Based Youth Ministry*, 34 (see chap. 1, n. 1).

24. Ibid., 41, 70.

25. Hersch, *A Tribe Apart*, 19.

As marketers honed their capacity to manipulate culture through consumable products, this tribal separation began earlier and ended later. Children began to mimic the styles and values of adolescent celebrities in elementary grades and even in preschool. By the end of the twentieth century, "extended adolescents" and "emerging adults" were persisting in adolescent life patterns into their twenties and thirties.[26]

How did twentieth-century churches respond to these cultural trends?

## The Rise of Age-Focused Ministries

As teenage subculture took on a power and identity all its own between the Roaring Twenties and the Vietnam War, the church was seen by many to be inherently irrelevant, boring, and out of touch with the modern and youthful world of adolescents.[27] In some cases the church's faith had become deeply entwined with the cultural and social traditions of previous generations, so entwined that, from the perspective of some Christian leaders, the emerging generation of adolescents might not find Christianity to be meaningful. In this context well-intentioned Christian leaders developed parachurch organizations, groups that engaged in organized Christian endeavors outside the direct influence of local churches, to evangelize students in ways that were intended to be more palatable to teenagers.

In the decades following the Second World War, Young Life, Youth for Christ, and similar ministries relied increasingly on professional youth workers to attract high-school students. By the 1960s and 1970s, local churches were imitating these parachurch ministries, hiring professional youth ministers whose primary purpose was to engage adolescents.[28] "We who did youth

---

26. This persistence of adolescent traits into an individual's twenties and thirties has been termed "extended adolescence" and has been associated in some research with a "quarterlife crisis." This term was popularized by Abby Wilner and Alexandra Robbins in their book *Quarterlife Crisis* (New York: Tarcher, 2001).

27. C. Clark, "The Missional Approach to Youth Ministry," in *Four Views of Youth Ministry and the Church,* ed. M. Senter III (Grand Rapids, Mich.: Zondervan, 2001), 82.

28. Mark Senter III rightly notes that some churches began to call youth ministers in the mid-1950s. However, this phenomenon did not become widespread until the 1960s and 1970s. Cf. M. Senter III, *The Coming Revolution in Youth Ministry* (Wheaton, Ill.:

ministry took the Youth for Christ and Young Life models," veteran youth worker Jim Burns has noted, "and brought them into the church."[29]

## The Release of Parental Responsibility

What these well-intended ministry models spawned in many congregations was a church culture mirroring the generational gap of the broader culture. Rather than healing ruptured connections between the generations, significant numbers of churches unintentionally welcomed, and perhaps even widened, the chasm between children and parents. At a time when cultural pressures had already alienated children from their parents, church ministries increasingly relied on age-segmented ministries to attract and to entertain students. As the locus of these ministries transitioned from parachurch to church-sponsored groups, the focus shifted from evangelizing nonbelieving students to retaining churched students.[30]

> Inspired by parachurch youth ministries from the 1950s, . . . ministries of distraction keep youth moving from one activity to the next. . . . It's a Nickelodeon approach to youth ministry that seeks to appeal to kids' propensity for fun and recreation. This is how churches respond to youth who cry, "Church is boring!" It's the ministry of excitement, discipleship through fun, culture-friendly, "Christian-lite" events. Like parents who pop in a video to entertain the kids when relatives arrive, the idea is to keep the young people from running out, to keep them in the general vicinity of the church, to keep them happy until they're mature enough to join the congregation.[31]

Victor, 1992), 142; D. Robbins, *This Way to Youth Ministry* (Grand Rapids, Mich.: Zondervan, 2004), 440–41.

29. W. Zorba, "Class of '00," *Christianity Today* (February 1997): 21.

30. Chap Clark has presented and defended this hypothesis in several contexts, including "Missional Approach," cited above.

31. M. Yaconelli, *Contemplative Youth Ministry* (Grand Rapids, Mich.: Zondervan, 2006), 44–45.

And thus, youth groups developed their own distinct expressions of Christian community, disconnected from the faith of their mothers and fathers.

By the end of the twentieth century, these patterns of ministry had become so widespread that they had reshaped not only youth ministry but also ministries to children and preschoolers. Ever-increasing percentages of parents released responsibility for their children's spiritual formation to professional ministers. In this way, the one-eared Mickey Mouse was born and metamorphosed into an octopus without a brain.

## Understanding Family Ministry

At the beginning of the twenty-first century, however, there is much reason for hope. Dozens of pastors and professors have glimpsed the problems highlighted here. Increasing numbers of parents and ministers have concluded that maybe the octopus wasn't the best model of ministry after all. "After decades of departmentalizing and compartmentalizing members of the family," Marv Penner has admitted, "the church is realizing that maybe it's time to start putting the family back together again."[32] These realizations have frequently been peppered with phrases like *family-integrated ministry, family-focused ministry, family-driven ministry, family-friendly ministry, ministry-integrated family focus,* or simply *family ministry.*

The problem is, though, that there has been no widespread agreement about what family ministry looks like in real life. There has been even less agreement about specific models of family ministry. And if you happen to ask the question, "Exactly how do I implement a family ministry in my church?"—well, prepare yourself for a lot of blank stares.

These blank stares reveal the paucity of practical tools available to help church leaders as they seek to implement family ministries in their congregations. And that's why this book is so important. Throughout the remainder of *Perspectives on Family Ministry*, we will look together at the dominant working

---

32. M. Penner, *Youth Worker's Guide to Parent Ministry* (Grand Rapids, Mich.: Zondervan, 2003), 1.

models of family ministry, closely examining the strengths and weaknesses of each one. Perhaps most important of all, we'll consider how churches can effectively move toward these ministry models.

CHAPTER 4

# *Foundations for Family Ministry*

When asked for a step-by-step process for implementing family ministry, Mark DeVries jokingly provided this progression: "Try something. Fail. Try something else. Fail again. Try something else. Stumble on one thing that works. Repeat what works. Try something else. You get the idea."[1] Even as I appreciate this kind of honesty and good humor, church leaders desperately need more specific definitions and processes to guide them as they formulate family ministries for their churches. One prominent youth leader worded his plea for a practical definition of family-based ministry in this way:

> If someone knows a simple definition of family-based youth ministry, please send it right away. I've read (and enjoyed) most of the books written on the subject. In fact, I can still remember reading . . . *Family-Based Youth Ministry* the very week it was published. . . . However, I'm still looking for that simple definition and practical handle on family-based youth ministry.[2]

"Unlike other areas of ministry focus," Chap Clark has observed, "family ministry emerged without any sort of across-the-board

---

1. M. DeVries, "Focusing Youth Ministry Through the Family," in *Starting Right: Thinking Theologically About Youth Ministry,* ed. K. Dean, et al. (Grand Rapids, Mich.: Zondervan,, 2001), 152.

2. www.youthspecialties.com/articles/topics/family/family_based.php.

consensus of just what it is. . . . Because of this lack of a common perception of family ministry, people responsible for family ministry in churches are often confused and frustrated."[3] And no wonder! According to Clark, no fewer than three distinct fields of "family ministry" can be found among contemporary churches.

Clark suggests that some churches operate with a *therapeutic-counseling* understanding of family ministry. Therapeutic-counseling family ministry includes "any services provided by a church or church agency, whether by a helping professional or by a nonprofessional volunteer, which aim to strengthen the relationships between family members."[4] In this perspective the phrase "family ministry" describes church-based courses and seminars that strengthen intact families, coupled with crisis-intervention programs to salvage troubled families. This was the form of family ministry promoted in the 1970s and 1980s in books by Oscar Feucht and Diana Garland. Although I concede that every church should provide programs to salvage and strengthen families, these programs alone cannot constitute a church's "family ministry." Think of it this way: Suppose your church provides counseling or therapy for troubled youth. You might view such programs as *one aspect of* your church's youth ministry, but you probably wouldn't *define* these programs as your church's "youth ministry." In the same way, programs for families ought to constitute one segment of a church's service to families; but, apart from other functions, such programs shouldn't really be defined as a church's "family ministry." Family ministry must be more than the addition of one more ministry to the "octopus without a brain"; authentic family ministry requires the church to reorient *all* of its ministries.

Another perspective is the *church-as-family* understanding of family ministry. This definition emphasizes the responsibility of the church to function as a close-knit community of believers. Viewed in this way, "family ministry" refers to the church's concerted effort to connect members in family-like relationships, regardless of their marital, generational, or developmental

3. Clark, *Youth Worker's Handbook*, 13 (see chap. 1, n. 4).
4. D. Garland and D. Pancoast, *The Church's Ministry with Families* (Waco, Tx.: Word, 1990), 4.

circumstances. This approach places little emphasis on parental responsibilities and focuses instead on helping the church to *become* a family for all people. In theory this approach draws individual families closer by pulling the entire community of faith together. To be sure, God *has* called every congregation of believers to function as a family of faith for all sorts of people. Yet this perspective ultimately sidesteps the core issues in family ministry, issues such as, "How will the church equip parents and children to relate to one another?" and "How will the church challenge parents to become primary disciple-makers in their children's lives?" As Chap Clark admits, a church-as-family perspective "may actually push a young person away from his family. After all, how can a night of playing board games and talking by the fire hope to compete with one hundred energetic kids cutting loose?"[5]

A final approach to understanding family ministry is what Clark has dubbed the *nuclear-family perspective*. In this perspective, "the primary training ground for discipleship and spiritual formation is the nuclear family rather than the local church. . . . [The nuclear-family perspective includes] a transfer of responsibility for the bulk of discipleship training from the church to the home."[6] Although the models presented in this book reach far beyond ministry to nuclear families, this perspective is probably the closest to the ones that the contributors to this text practice in their churches.

After delineating these disparate definitions of family ministry, Chap Clark concludes that "there is not now, nor is there likely ever to be, an identifiable programmatic animal known as 'family ministry.'"[7] Perhaps he's right. Maybe family ministry will metamorphose so radically from place to place that it defies precise meaning. Yet, even if definitions of family ministry *do* remain a bit slippery, churches dare not continue to consign the Christian formation of their children to professional ministers. Specific models and structures for family ministry are desperately needed. Church leaders need to know how to plan ministries

---

5. Clark, *Youth Worker's Handbook*, 19.
6. Ibid., 16.
7. Ibid., 20.

that draw parents and children together instead of driving them apart (Mal 4:6; Luke 1:17). Congregations need practical ministry models guiding parents to embrace principal responsibility for their children's spiritual formation.

The reflections found in this book are different from so many others. The contributors to this volume do not merely discuss family ministry; they have *done* family ministry, and they're continuing to do family ministry. What readers will find in these pages is not another hypothesis or two from the proverbial ivory tower about how churches might theoretically do family ministry. Rather, they will gain wisdom from leaders who have fashioned workable models for family ministry in real-life churches. There is guidance in determining which models of family ministry might work best in individual congregations, along with specific strategies to maintain peace as ministries are reoriented to mesh with the family-ministry model that best fits one's church.

Which brings us to this book's perspective on the meaning of "family ministry," a definition that's far from the final word but one that's rooted in the research and reflections of many family-ministry practitioners.

---

### Defining Family Ministry

This book defines *family ministry* as "the process of intentionally and persistently realigning a congregation's proclamation and practices so that parents are acknowledged, trained, and held accountable as the persons primarily responsible for the discipleship of their children." What would you add to this definition? What would you delete?

---

## Family Ministry: A Definition

When the phrase *family ministry* appears in this book, here is what is meant: "the process of intentionally and persistently realigning a congregation's proclamation and practices so that parents are acknowledged, trained, and held accountable as the persons primarily responsible for the discipleship of their children." Such a perspective does *not* absolve the church of its responsibility to partner with persons from every age grouping and social background in the task of discipleship (including divorced persons, single mothers, never-married singles, children from single-parent households, and children of pre-Christian parents).[8] This definition recognizes that God designed families to serve as the foremost framework for children's spiritual formation. The family is a normative context for the discipleship of children. Every Christian parent is, therefore, responsible to engage personally in the formation of his or her child's faith.

This definition also recognizes that "family ministry" requires far more than a slight tweaking of present paradigms of youth or children's ministry. Several popular ministry models whose titles include the word *family* fall short because they treat *family ministry* as nothing more than a fresh form of *youth ministry*. While the intent of these models is commendable, family ministry is *not* merely one more method for doing youth ministry. Family ministry is also *not* another church program that a pastor can add to the present array of programs. Such a programmatic approach, while well intended, is not what this book defines as "family ministry." Family ministry represents a fundamentally different way of doing church. Full-fledged family ministry entails more than the addition of one more purpose or program. It requires persistent and intentional reorientation of the entire church's perspective on the processes of evangelism and discipleship.

## *Models for Family Ministry*

How are churches doing family ministry? As I have worked with pastors and churches to develop new ministry paradigms, I have observed three workable models for family ministry that fit within the definition formulated for this book.

---

8. Among early Christians, the church in general and elders in particular were responsible to include orphans in the life of the congregation: "If any child among the Christians is an orphan, it is well that if any brother has no children, he should adopt the orphan in place of children. . . . And you who are overseers: Watch carefully over the orphan's upbringing that they lack nothing! When a virgin girl is of age, give her in marriage to a brother. As a boy is brought up, let him learn a craft so that, when he becomes a man, he will earn a worthy wage" (*Didascalia Apostolorum* 17).

## Family-Integrated Ministry

First, there's the *family-integrated ministry model*. This model is also known as a *family-driven* or *family discipleship* approach. Several years ago, Malan Nel advocated a position similar to the family-integrated model in South African churches, using the term *inclusive-congregational ministry*.[9] Family-integrated ministry is by far the most radical model. In a family-integrated church, all age-graded classes and events are eliminated. That's right: *No* youth group, *no* children's church, *no* grade-segmented Sunday school classes. Generations learn and worship together, and parents bear primary responsibility for the evangelism and discipleship of their children.

Voddie Baucham, pastor of Grace Family Baptist Church and author of *Family-Driven Faith*, has been one of the most vocal defenders of family integration. Other promoters and practitioners of family-integrated ministry include Doug Phillips at Vision Forum and Scott Brown at the National Center for Family-Integrated Churches. One of the most articulate recent proponents of this perspective has been Paul Renfro, director of the Alliance for Church and Family Reformation.

Here's how the National Center for Family-Integrated Churches has described the structure and values of a family-integrated congregation:

> The biblical family is a scripturally-ordered household of parents, children, and sometimes others (such as singles, widows, divorcees, or grandparents), forming the God-ordained building blocks of the church (2 Tim 4:19). We . . . reject the church's implementation of modern individualism by fragmenting the family through age-graded, peer-oriented, and special-interest classes, thus preventing rather than promoting family unity.[10]

---

9. M. Nel, "Inclusive-Congregational Approach," in Senter, *Four Views of Youth Ministry*, 29.

10. www.visionforumministries.org/projects/ncfic/a_biblical_confession_for_unit.aspx.

In a family-integrated congregation, each scripturally ordered household is a building block; together these building blocks constitute the local church.

## Family-Based Ministry

Second, there's the model that's been termed *family-based*. In the family-based ministry model, no radical changes occur in the church's internal structure. The congregation still maintains youth ministry, children's ministry, singles ministry, and so on. What makes the practices of these churches different from the octopus-without-a-brain templates of the twentieth century is the focus of each ministry, coupled with the addition of some intergenerational curriculum, activities, or events. Students may still experience worship and small groups in peer gatherings, separated from other generations. Yet each ministry sponsors events and learning experiences that are intentionally designed to draw generations together. Mark DeVries pioneered this approach and presented its implications in his book *Family-Based Youth Ministry*.

One way to envision the family-based approach would be to think of a sunflower. Each petal remains separate, yet all the petals come together at the central disk. In the same way, each ministry in a family-based congregation remains separate. Central to the congregation's mission, however, is the expectation that every ministry will consistently plan events and learning experiences that draw families and generations together.

## Family-Equipping Ministry

To describe the third and final approach, I have coined the term *family-equipping ministry*. In this model, many semblances of age-organized ministry remain intact. In some cases the family-equipping church might even retain a youth minister or a children's minister. Yet church leaders plan every ministry to champion the place of parents as primary disciple-makers in their children's lives, asking, "What is best for families?" at every level of the church's ministry. At the same time, parents recognize the church as a community called to participate actively in the discipleship of all believers, including children. The church equips parents to disciple their children, and the parents recognize the church as an active partner in this process. Whereas family-based churches develop intergenerational events and activities within current structures, family-equipping ministry reworks the church's entire structure to call parents to disciple their children at every level of the church's work. Every aspect of the congregation's life consciously cochampions the church's ministry *and* the parent's responsibility.

While redeveloping curriculum in the School of Leadership and Church Ministry at The Southern Baptist Theological Seminary, Randy Stinson and I developed the theoretical framework for this model and then searched for churches that were already engaging in the practices we had described. In the process we discovered dozens of like-minded professors and practitioners, including Jay Strother at Brentwood Baptist Church in Tennessee, Brian Haynes at Kingsland Baptist Church in Texas, and Steve Wright at Providence Baptist Church in North Carolina. The family-equipping approach is similar to the model that Ben Freudenburg calls *family-centered/church-supported*.[11] Steve Wright has referred to this model as a process of *cochampioning* the church and the home.[12] At Rock Harbor Church, near Los Angeles, Michelle Anthony describes this approach as *family-empowered*.[13]

To envision the family-equipping model in action, imagine a river with large stones jutting through the surface of the water. The river represents children's growth and development. One riverbank signifies the church, and the other riverbank connotes the family. Both banks are necessary for the river to flow forward with focus and power. Unless both riverbanks support the child's development, what is likely to be created is the destructive power of a deluge instead of the constructive possibilities of a river. The

---

11. See B. Freudenberg, *The Family-Friendly Church* (Loveland, Colo.: Group, 1998). Some aspects of Freudenberg's model are also similar to Mark DeVries' family-based approach.

12. For this term here and throughout this book, see Wright and Graves, *reThink* (see chap. 2, n. 28).

13. M. Anthony, "New Models of Family Ministry," North American Professors of Christian Education, 2008.

stones that guide and redirect the river currents represent milestones or rites of passage that mark the passing of key thresholds in the child's life—points of development that the church and families celebrate together.

### Relating the Models to One Another

None of these ministry models is absolutely exclusive of the others. Each one is likely to overlap with one or two other models (see diagram). The worship celebration in a family-integrated congregation could look a lot like the intergenerational worship services practiced in family-equipping churches. Much of the programming in a family-based congregation will likely look similar to the programmatic models of previous decades, though family-based churches will involve parents in as many events as possible.[14] There could certainly be similarities between parent-training programs in family-equipping and family-based congregations. Still, each model of family ministry represents a distinct and identifiable approach to the challenge of drawing the home and the church into a life-transforming partnership.

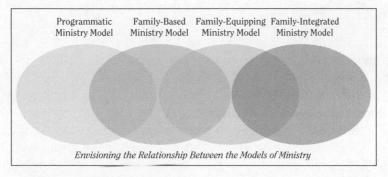

| Programmatic | Family-Based | Family-Equipping | Family-Integrated |
| Ministry Model | Ministry Model | Ministry Model | Ministry Model |

*Envisioning the Relationship Between the Models of Ministry*

### Finding the Common Ground

My goal is not to convince readers that one of these models is better than the others. What I *do* want to do is to equip them with the knowledge needed to discern which model might work best in their congregation and to provide them with practical

---

14. M. DeVries, et al., Youth Ministry Architects Web site: www.ymarchitects.com/resources.html.

plans to implement that model. I believe that every church is called to some form of family ministry. At the same time, I know there is not one single model of family ministry that will work in every community of faith. That is why I encourage ministry leaders in every church to consider all three of these models and then to pursue God's particular calling for their congregation with passion and joy.

Despite deep-rooted differences in their ministry models, the participants in this discussion do share a triad of fundamental assumptions about the church's ministry. In the first place, all agree that *Scripture is the supreme and sufficient standard for how to do ministry.* Scripture is not simply one more source of authority alongside organizational psychologies, statistical correlations, and other social-scientific claims. The Word of God—which is to say, God enfleshed in Jesus Christ, whose identity is impeccably revealed to us in the pages of Holy Scripture—provides the regulative template for Christian faith and practice.

How secular diagnostic and statistical manuals define family relationships can never become determinative for ministry praxis. Whether a method seems to work from a human perspective is beside the point. How ministries have been done in the past is significant only insomuch as these past ministries have conformed to the patterns preserved in Scripture. The Word of God stands alone as the first, final, and sufficient word.

In the second place, each contributor also recognizes that *God has called parents—and especially fathers—to take personal responsibility for the Christian formation of their children.* Neither I nor any other contributor is claiming that parents should never partner with church ministers to form their children's faith. What we *are* claiming is that, from the perspective of God's Word, parents must embrace primary responsibility for their children's spiritual maturity.

In the shadow of Mount Sinai, God "established a testimony in Jacob, . . . which He commanded our fathers to teach to their children so that a future generation . . . might know" (Ps 78:5–6). The apostle Paul commanded fathers to train their children "in the training and instruction of the Lord" (Eph 6:4). As far as I know, these divine paradigms for spiritual formation have never shifted.

In the early twentieth century, a journalist named G. K. Chesterton offered these comments about the British and American jury system:

> The trend of our epoch up to this time has been consistently towards specialism and professionalism. We tend to have trained soldiers because they fight better, trained singers because they sing better, trained dancers because they dance better, specially instructed laughers because they laugh better, and so on and so on. . . . [Yet] our civilization has decided, and very justly decided, that determining the guilt or innocence of men is a thing too important to be trusted to trained men. When it wishes for light upon that awful matter, it asks men who know no more law than I know, but who can feel the things that I felt in the jury box. When it wants a library catalogued, or the solar system discovered, or any trifle of that kind, it uses up its specialists. But when it wishes anything done which is really serious, it collects twelve of the ordinary men standing round. The same thing was done, if I remember right, by the Founder of Christianity.[15]

A similar statement might be made regarding the training of children in Christian faith. Though professionals may partner with parents in this task, such a vast and serious undertaking as a child's discipleship is too significant to be relinquished completely to professionals. God has selected specific, ordinary people for this assignment, and these people are known as "Dad" and "Mom." The primary formation of a child's faith is not a job for specialists. It is a job for parents.[16]

There is a third assumption that each contributor shares: *The generations need one another.* Alongside the drift toward

---

15. G. K. Chesterton, *Tremendous Trifles* (Charleston, S.C.: BiblioBazaar, 2006), 51–54.

16. G. Barna, *Revolutionary Parenting* (Carol Stream, Ill.: Tyndale House, 2007), 12.

surrendering discipleship to professional ministers, another trend has developed too: Church programs have tended to become so radically age segmented that, in many congregations, persons from different generations rarely if ever interact with one another in the context of the faith community. Such segmentation isn't merely a *church* problem, either. It has become characteristic of society as a whole. Mary Pipher put it most poignantly when she pointed out,

> A great deal of America's moral sickness comes from age segregation. If ten 14-year-olds are grouped together, they will form a *Lord of the Flies* culture with its competitiveness and meanness. But if ten people aged two to 80 are grouped together, they will fall into a natural age hierarchy that nurtures and teaches them all. For our own mental and societal health, we need to reconnect the age groups.[17]

To this, I would add a single sentence: For the health of our *churches,* we must reconnect the age groups. "What kids need from adults is not just rides, pizza, chaperones, and discipline," Patricia Hersch acknowledged in a study of adolescent culture. "They need the telling of stories, the close ongoing contact so they can learn and be accepted. If nobody is there to talk to, it is difficult to get the lessons of your own life so that you are adequately prepared to do the next thing."[18]

In the late 1990s, a syphilis outbreak in a small southern city exposed an underworld of casual sex and substance abuse involving hundreds of adolescents. In the aftermath of this epidemic, reporters interviewed more than a dozen parents and participants. These families' descriptions of their evening routines provided a snapshot of this deep-seated societal fragmentation: "We was [sic] a very close family when they was [sic] younger," one father claimed. "Still are." Yet here's how this father described his family's time together in their home:

---

17. M. Pipher, "The New Generation Gap," *USA Weekend* (March 21, 1999): Retrieved from www.usaweekend.com/99_issues/990321/990321pipher.html.

18. Hersch, *A Tribe Apart*, 364 (see chap. 3, n. 52).

FOUNDATIONS FOR FAMILY MINISTRY — **49**

Well, we got TVs in every room of the house. I watch my programs. My wife watches her programs in another room in the house. You know, the kids watch it or play . . . their video games. . . . Much of the time that we had in the house together was not together.

*"Much of the time that we had in the house together was not together."* The same might be said for families in many churches. Children's programs, youth programs, and adult programs occur in isolation from one another. Churches somehow expect family members to become integrated with one another at home even as they model disintegration in their activities and organizational structures. "In the past," intergenerational specialist Holly Allen has pointed out, "spending family time together and going to church were the same thing. Now, family time and church time are not compatible ideas, because families are rarely together when they are at church."[19]

The biblical authors, however, assumed the presence of generational connections that equipped children and youth to gain wisdom from older generations. In the divine law, God declared to His people, "You are to rise in the presence of the elderly and honor the old." Then, He linked this respect to His own sacred identity: "Fear your God; I am the LORD" (Lev 19:32). From the perspective of the Proverbs, it was "your father's instruction, and . . . your mother's teaching" that guided a child to follow God (Prov 1:8; see 3:1; 6:20). When Moses prepared for his passage into the next life, the leader of Israel commanded Joshua to gather the generations together—men, women, and children—so that "children . . . may listen and learn to fear the LORD" (Deut 31:12).

There *is* something to be said for recognizing distinctions in the developmental capabilities of children, youth, and adults. Yet part of the scandal of the cross of Christ is the fact that persons who rub shoulders in the shadow of the cross are people the world would never dream of mingling together (1 Cor 1:23–29; 12:13; Gal 3:28; Eph 2:14; Col 3:11). In a culture that has severed vital ties between the generations, this should include the

---

19. Wright and Graves, *reThink*, 103.

meaningful and intentional commingling of the generations at church.

The contributors to this book do differ when it comes to how often and under what circumstances the church's activities and learning experiences ought to bring the generations together. Yet all of them agree that complete and continual segmentation of the generations does not adequately reflect God's plan for God's people. Churches must intentionally create contexts that equip dissimilar generations to live their faith together.

## "Things Are Different Now"

"This is Wednesday night *youth group*. We don't *do* Bibles here," the high-school senior said to me a decade ago. "We're here to have fun."

"Well," I replied once I had located my vocal cords, "things are different now."

At the time, I didn't realize how right I was.

In the space of a couple of centuries, the generations have drifted so far apart that recalibrating an entire congregation to engage in family ministry appears radical, perhaps even impossible. The majority of parents have handed over the task of discipling their children to professional ministers. Churches have constructed entire ministry models on foundations that strain family structures instead of drawing family members together.

Things *are* different now.

Still, I'm hopeful.

I'm hopeful because I see a beautiful opportunity that towers far above these cultural transitions. It's the possibility that churches will become contexts where the generations are drawn together instead of being driven apart, places where the hearts of fathers turn anew toward the hearts of their children, communities where nonbelievers cannot help but glimpse the glorious presence of something that's absent from their homes.

The family ministry models presented in this book will not pull the generations together. I know that. These models are merely tools, constructed by well-meaning but imperfect people.

What, then, is my desire for this book? Simply this: That God may refine and use these less-than-perfect tools as He shapes His churches to reflect more perfectly the character of Jesus Christ.

| | Programmatic Ministry Model | Family-Based Ministry Model | Family-Equipping Ministry Model | Family-Integrated Ministry Model |
|---|---|---|---|---|
| **What does this model look like in the local church?** | Ministries are organized in separate "silos," with little consistent intergenerational interaction. "Family ministry," when it exists, is one more program. The program may provide training, intervention, or activities for families. In scheduling programs, churches may deliberately seek to be sensitive to family's needs and schedules. | Church's programmatic structure remains unchanged, but each separate ministry plans and programs in ways that intentionally draw generations together and encourage parents to take part in the discipleship of their children and youth. | Although age-organized programs and events still exist, the church is completely restructured to draw the generations together, equipping parents, championing their role as primary disciple-makers, and holding them accountable to fulfill this role. | The church eliminates age-segregated programs and events. All or nearly all programs and events are multigenerational, with a strong focus on parents' responsibility to evangelize and to disciple their own children. |
| **What other approaches might be included in this ministry model?** | Therapeutic-Counseling Family Ministry (Chap Clark)[1]<br><br>Church-Centered/Home-Supported Ministry (Ben Freudenburg)[2]<br><br>Family-Sensitive Ministry (Michelle Anthony)[3] | Family-Friendly Youth Ministry; Family-Focused Youth Ministry (Dave Rahn)[4]<br><br>Family-Based Youth Ministry (Mark DeVries)[5]<br><br>Family-Friendly Ministry (Michelle Anthony)[6] | Youth-Focused Family Ministry; Youth-Friendly Family Ministry (Dave Rahn)[7]<br><br>Home-Centered/Church-Supported Ministry (Ben Freudenburg)[8]<br><br>Cochampion Model (Steve Wright)[9]<br><br>Family-Empowered Ministry (Michelle Anthony)[10] | Family Discipleship Churches (Alliance for Church and Family Reformation)[11]<br><br>Family-Centered Ministry (Michelle Anthony)[12]<br><br>Inclusive-Congregational Ministry (Malan Nel)[13] |

1. Clark, *Youth Worker's Handbook.*    2. Freudenberg, *Family-Friendly Church.*    3. Anthony, "New Models of Family Ministry."    4. D. Rahn, "Parafamily Youth Ministry," in *Group* (May/June 1996): archive.youthministry.com/details.asp?ID=1701.    5. M. DeVries with E. Palmer, *Family-Based Youth Ministry* rev. ed. (Downers Grove, Ill.: InterVarsity, 2004).    6. Anthony, "New Models of Family Ministry."    7. Rahn, "Parafamily Youth Ministry."    8. Freudenberg, *Family-Friendly Church.*    9. Wright and Graves, *reThink.*    10. Anthony, "New Models of Family Ministry."    11. www.gracefamilybaptist.net/GFBC_/Alliance.html.    12. Anthony, "New Models of Family Ministry."    13. Nel, "Inclusive-Congregational Approach," 29.

# PART 2

# How Churches Are Doing Family Ministry

*by Paul Renfro,
Brandon Shields, and Jay Strother*

# CHAPTER 5

# Family-Integrated Ministry
## FAMILY-DRIVEN FAITH
### Paul Renfro

*Pastor of Discipleship*
*Grace Family Baptist Church*

My desire to serve in full-time ministry began in a place you probably wouldn't expect: on the basketball court. At six feet nine inches tall, I had the privilege of playing basketball with a sports ministry team known as Athletes in Action. For three years I traveled the world, proclaiming the gospel at halftime presentations, in school assemblies, and at summer camps. I knew I was investing in eternity. At the same time, I believed then, and I still believe now, that the local church is God's primary vehicle for the expansion of His kingdom. This desire to serve God in local churches eventually led me to enroll in seminary.

When I began my first semester of seminary, I envisioned a future filled with fruitful and fulfilling ministry in local congregations of believers. That vision carried me through the rigors of New Testament Greek and systematic theology. After graduation, I began my first pastorate in a small church in Ohio.

That's where my glorious vision of ministry collided with reality.

For two decades, I served local churches as a senior pastor, as a minister to singles, as a bivocational elder, and as a church planter. While a singles minister in a larger congregation in Texas, the youth minister and I agonized over the amount of time we spent oiling the organizational machinery of our particular, age-segregated ministry areas instead of being involved in lasting changes in people's lives.

"I spend 90 percent of my time in administrative tasks, with little time left to invest in people's lives," the youth minister lamented. The ministry contexts changed from time to time, but the struggle remained the same: So much time oiling the organizational machinery, so little time to invest in authentic discipleship, and so few results proportionate to the efforts of the churches and their ministers. After nearly twenty years of watching this pattern play out in churches, I began to consider walking away from vocational ministry.

I'm so glad that I didn't.

I didn't know it at the time, but I was standing at that moment on the threshold of the most fulfilling ministry of my life, ministry in a family-integrated church.

---

### What Constitutes a "Family-Integrated Church"?

According to the National Center for Family-Integrated Churches, "we affirm that the biblical family is a scripturally ordered household of parents, children, and sometimes others (such as singles, widows, divorcees, or grandparents), forming the God-ordained building blocks of the church (2 Tim 4:19). We . . . reject the church's implementation of modern individualism by fragmenting the family through age-graded, peer-oriented, and special-interest classes, thus preventing rather than promoting family unity."[1]

---

## A Clean Break from Age-Segregated Ministry

What is a family-integrated church? Here's how Voddie Baucham has described the family-integrated movement:

> The family-integrated church movement is easily distinguishable in its insistence on integration as an ecclesiological principle. . . . Our church has no youth ministers, children's ministers, or nursery. We do not divide families into

---

1. "A Biblical Confession for Uniting Church and Family": www.visionforumministries.org/projects/ncfic/a_biblical_confession_for_unit.aspx.

component parts. We do not separate the mature women from the young teenage girls who need their guidance. We do not separate the toddler from his parents during worship. In fact, we don't even do it in Bible study. We see the church as a family of families.[2]

In 2006, I was privileged to become a founding elder in a family-integrated congregation in a suburb of Houston. This church began with a conscious focus on evaluating every method in light of Scripture. On the first Sunday, a plurality of elders gathered with five families in one elder's home. Two months later, the church had grown to more than ninety regular attenders, forcing us to find a larger facility. Family-integrated church was unlike anything that anyone in this group had ever encountered! Two years later, hundreds of people gather every Sunday to worship together at Grace Family Baptist Church.

The church's leadership structure is simple and biblical. Several elders focus on studying the Scriptures, praying, and shepherding the flock. Deacons oversee the church's day-to-day operations and make certain that the congregation provides for people's needs.

The church calendar is simple too: There's one worship celebration on Sunday morning, followed by a fellowship meal. Small groups meet during the week to study. Each month, the men's meeting gathers with the distinct goal of training men to be spiritual leaders. This simple schedule provides time for families to live life together, so that parents can disciple their children and families can practice hospitality toward those inside and outside the community of faith.

## *Worshiping Together, the Highlight of the Week*

In this family-integrated congregation, Sunday worship is the highlight of the week. There are no professional greeters standing at the door to divide families by directing each family member to a different destination. Children, youth, and adults

---

2. For this quotation as well as a fuller description of family-integrated ministry, see V. Baucham, *Family Driven Faith* (Wheaton, Ill.: Crossway, 2007), 191–95.

spontaneously greet anyone who arrives, working together to help people bring in their food for the fellowship meal. Ladies and girls organize food for lunch. A couple of men—which, from our perspective, includes teenaged males—set up sound equipment. A worship team rehearses the morning's music; a young man types catechetical questions into the computer; teenage ladies work at the greeting table. At every level, adults and children engage in service and fellowship together.

It's a beautiful sight seeing whole families seated together. Babies, toddlers, preschoolers, children, youth, single adults, parents, grandparents—all of them, gathered in anticipation, preparing to worship their heavenly Father. During the time of greeting, visitors are informed that we are accustomed to children in the service. At the same time, we make them aware that, if children choose to act up and disturb others in the worship service, parents are welcome to take the children out to deal with them. Family-integrated churches promote active parenting!

There are so many great benefits to families worshiping together. Worshiping as a family with the gathered church communicates to children that worshiping God is something much broader than their peers or their family. Children mature spiritually as they experience authentic fellowship with God's people instead of being subjected to glorified child care. They soak up far more than many people might think as they watch their parents worshiping, praying, listening, and humbling themselves week by week. These experiences build memories of worship with their particular family and with the family of God that will remain with them throughout their lives. Family members enjoy the same worship experience, and they are able to discuss these experiences together.

In our particular congregation, we work through a prayer guide in the bulletin early in the worship service. This guide lists five families in our church and government officials as well as an unreached people group. The bulletin also provides the needed tools for fathers to lead their families in worship at home, even if they've never led family worship before. The worshiper finds a hymn of the week, some catechism questions, and the prayer guide. There are also New Testament and Old Testament readings that can be broken into smaller portions to read during the week.

An older boy leads the congregation in several catechism questions and answers. In the not-too-distant past, parents used catechisms to teach their children key theological beliefs. In a short time children memorized dozens of theological truths. This time-tested method still works.

After catechism, the congregation joins in a blend of hymns and contemporary songs with solid theological content, interspersed with biblical readings by the men of the church. Our men are known to hope that their assigned week doesn't fall in the middle of a genealogy or in Joshua's lists of tribal allotments!

Expository preaching, working through books of the Bible to glean the whole counsel of God, follows the singing. Sermons are geared for adults, yet we're amazed at what children get out of these messages. Over and over, parents tell us how their children have referred back to something that was mentioned in a sermon. It isn't necessary to "dumb down" the message nearly as much as our culture claims we must. Since family members hear the same message, families are able to discuss the message at home.

After the sermon the congregation prepares for Lord's Supper. Each father gathers his family, guiding them toward reflection, repentance, and reconciliation before a time of prayer. Those without families gather with a family, or they can pray alone. Worship through tithes and offering follows and, if requested, elders pray for needs in keeping with Jas 5:14–16.

After worship, many hands are on deck to prepare the weekly fellowship lunch. Being Baptists, we hold strong convictions about eating every time we meet! Actually, this is not simply a Baptist tradition, for it follows the apostolic pattern described in Acts 2:46.

Since church members come from all over the metropolitan area, it makes sense to provide extended opportunities for members and visitors to fellowship. Men and boys set up tables and chairs, while ladies and girls finish the food preparations. Everyone has a place to serve. Last Sunday I watched a teenage girl work alongside her three-year-old sister—recently adopted from Russia—and a six-year-old boy to prepare the drinks. The preparations and the meal provide wonderful opportunities for ministry and for informal mentoring, in keeping with Titus 2:1–8. To listen in on a few conversations is to discover a rich range of topics, moving from the day's sermon, current events, child training, and home education to business, theology, history, home repairs, family discipleship, and hurricane evacuation strategies! Believers receive wisdom and counsel from one another. Visitors get to know church members. Girls hold babies and help mothers care for their young children. It's an immeasurable blessing to see relationships blossom between different ages!

From the perspective of an elder, the most difficult task is not generating interest in fellowship so much as trying to bring it to a close. Even after the doors are locked, many church members linger in the parking lot or continue the fellowship in their homes.

## Training Members in the Family-Integrated Church

Weekly small groups provide further instruction and fellowship. Members meet in homes to study specific topics including biblical surveys, spiritual disciplines, marriage, and child training. As on Sunday mornings, families remain together so that they learn and grow together. Children look forward to our small groups and listen attentively, even taking notes and reading Scriptures. Children learn much as they hear wiser believers discussing theological questions and spiritual matters. Sometimes children contribute to the conversations too! I've seen children correctly answer questions like, "What is the difference between a literal translation like the English Standard Version and a dynamic equivalent translation like the New International Version?" or "What did George Muller learn about the relationship between meditation and prayer?" Once again they absorb more than we realize!

## Training Fathers to Lead

A monthly meeting for men rounds out the church's schedule. Attending this meeting is a vital responsibility for men in our church. We don't have to emphasize this responsibility very much, though, because men *want* to attend.

These men understand that we live in the midst of a battle for biblical manhood. So often, men mention that they never knew how to lead their own families because they never had a role model. Rare is the man whose father has discipled him. Yet we've found that most Christian men will rise to the challenge if they are equipped, encouraged, held accountable, and provided with examples.

When the men gather together, they worship, share testimonies, ask questions about family discipleship, encourage each other, and pray in small groups. There's great encouragement to know other men are running the same race. Each month elders also provide practical instruction on everything from how to love your wife to how to lead family worship. Men must feed themselves in order to feed their families, so each year eight or nine books are also assigned.

## Men's Discipleship and the Myth of Adolescence

When boys turned twelve in Jewish culture, they began to be viewed as bearing responsibilities associated with manhood. The Scriptures show Jesus at age twelve, sitting with older teachers in the temple, "listening to them and asking them questions" (Luke 2:46). Unfortunately, in contemporary culture, acceptance of extended immaturity, especially for males, has replaced the ancient expectation of moving toward adult responsibilities.

In family-integrated churches we do not encourage the cultural phenomena known as "adolescence"—a phenomenon that is, as it is perceived and practiced in our particular culture, only a couple of generations old. David Black, author of *The Myth of Adolescence,* summarizes the problem in this way:

According to the Bible, the teen era is not a "time-out" between childhood and adulthood. It is not primarily a time of horseplay, of parties, of sports, of games. It is not a period of temporary insanity. The Bible treats teens as responsible young adults, and so should we. Paul told Timothy, a young man, to "be an example for other believers in your speech, behavior, love, faith, and purity" (1 Tim 4:12).

Though still young, Timothy was to speak, act, love, believe, and relate to the opposite sex in such a way that others would look at his life and want to be just like him.[3]

Simply put, there is no biblical basis for an artificial period of immaturity between childhood and adulthood. If we expect immaturity and irresponsibility in those years, that is exactly what we will get. The opposite, however, is also true. In our congregation, we encourage fathers to celebrate their son's twelfth birthday with a manhood ceremony. For our young men, the teen years are intended to be productive years of learning to be a man.

One benefit of turning twelve is that these young men can finally attend the monthly men's meeting. Many of them have eagerly anticipated this rite of passage since they were nine or ten, and by developing relationships with a community of men, they gain a multitude of male role models and strong reinforcements for what their fathers teach at home.

## What's Distinctive about Family-Integrated Churches?

Family-integrated churches are not all identical. They are found in a variety of denominations, with differing beliefs and practices. For example, in North Carolina, there is Antioch Community Church, where J. Mark Fox pastors, and Hope Baptist Church, led by Scott Brown. In Monee, Illinois, the Family of Faith is shepherded by Henry Reyenga. Near Houston is our congregation, Grace Family Baptist Church. In the northwestern United States, there is Household of Faith Community Church, guided by Gregg Harris. These are just a very few of many such churches found all over the country. Despite such a

---

3. D. Black, *The Myth of Adolescence.*

range of locations and congregations, there are three distinctive commitments that every family-integrated church shares: First is a commitment to age-integrated ministry. Second, there is a commitment to evangelism and discipleship in and through the home. And third, the churches are committed to calling church leaders who meet the biblical qualification of managing their homes in a godly way (1 Tim 3:4; Titus 1:6). Consider carefully each of these three commitments:

## Commitment to Age-Integrated Ministry

The most obvious distinctive of a family-integrated church is age-integrated ministry. Family integration means there is no age-segregated Sunday school, youth group, or children's ministry. Different generations worship together, learn together, serve together, and fellowship together. Family-integrated churches follow the biblical pattern of intergenerational worship and learning (Deut 29:10–11; Josh 8:35; 2 Chron 20:13; Joel 2:16).

Age-integration creates a network of meaningful multi-generational relationships. The apostle Paul specifically stated that mentoring relationships ought to occur between older and younger believers (Titus 2:1–8). Such integration allows godly men to mentor the sons of single mothers or the sons of mothers with husbands who are not yet believers. A biblical example of this pattern can be seen in the relationship of Paul with Timothy (1 Tim 1:2; 2 Tim 1:2; Acts 16:1). Integration also allows godly widows and more mature women to mentor young mothers, and it allows grandparents to develop relationships with younger families.

Age-integration promotes maturity. Proverbs 13:20 warns, "The one who walks with the wise will become wise, but a companion of fools will suffer harm." Placing peers together is a formula for deepening and perpetuating immaturity. Early Christians clearly recognized this truth. In one early church manual, here's the advice given to Christian parents:

> Don't give your children liberty that lets them set themselves against you as their parents! . . . If you do, they will end up running around with people their own age, cluster-

ing together and carousing. That's how they learn mischief; then, they find themselves caught up in mischief, and they fall into immorality.[4]

What a clear statement of what happens when adolescents' primary influences come from their peers. Intergenerational influences and age-integration, on the other hand, encourage healthy processes of maturation. Age-integration within each family also accelerates the deepening of family relationships. The more experiences a family shares together, the closer that family becomes. In such a context, hearts naturally will be turned toward each other (Mal 4:6).

## Commitment to Evangelism and Discipleship
## In and Through the Home

Family-integrated churches are committed to evangelism and discipleship in and through the home. Scripture clearly states that parents should be primary disciple-makers in their children's lives (Eph 6:1–4). Paul spoke directly to fathers, exhorting them to train up their children in the fear and admonition of the Lord. These New Testament admonitions were echoes of such Old Testament texts as Deuteronomy 6 and the seventy-eighth psalm. In family-integrated churches the father's role as spiritual leader is not an empty title. It is a serious, sacred task that the church equips him to pursue and holds him accountable to fulfill.

In the home, parents have constant opportunities to train their children to obey God's commands. When a child disobeys, parents can immediately discipline and instruct them in the way of Christ. Who is better able to discern the condition of their children's hearts and to know if true repentance has occurred than those who live with them every day?

The home is the best context for discipleship, and the family is also the best context for the evangelism of persons outside the church. That's how the apostle Paul evangelized in the first century AD:

---

4. *Didascalia Apostolorum* 22.

Paul's conversion approach to urban missions was family-centered. The households mentioned in the New Testament (Acts 16:15; 1 Cor 1:16; Gal 6:10) were not unlike the extended families and kinship ties found in Southern (frequently called "Third") world countries today, and Paul used these households to establish the faith in each area he evangelized.[5]

In the church's early centuries, missionaries evangelized households, and these households in turn evangelized other households.

How can a Christian household become a context for the evangelism of unbelievers? Through intentional hospitality, unbelieving visitors are able to observe the dynamics of a Christian family. When an unbelieving family eats with a family of believers and sees a loving family with respectful children, they glimpse a bright light in a dark culture.

In family-integrated churches we minister to our neighbors together as families, displaying traits that are severely lacking in our culture: *Family unity and industry*. Families in our church receive so many comments from people who are amazed at their children's maturity and wisdom. People are even more amazed when they see teenagers and parents who actually enjoy being together. This is such a rarity in today's world, but it is also a wonderful opportunity to tell people *why* we differ from the cultural norm. This becomes an opportunity for evangelizing unbelievers.

When it comes to discipleship, training men to disciple their families is a high priority in family-integrated churches. In our congregation the monthly men's meeting is the primary training time for men. We have established a church culture that calls men to lead. During worship services family prayer times are led by fathers, which emphasizes our belief that men are the shepherds of their families.

Even our membership process emphasizes expectations for family discipleship. Our membership covenant calls for a com-

---

5. R. Greenway and T. Monsma, *Cities: Missions' New Frontier* (Grand Rapids, Mich.: Baker, 2000), 41.

mitment to family worship and discipleship. Activities that integrate entire families provide implicit accountability for child training. Each spring a family conference brings encouragement and instruction for families.

From the perspective of church leadership, calling and equipping men to lead their families pays rich dividends, too. No one understood this better than a seventeenth-century Puritan named Richard Baxter:

> Get masters of families to do their duty, and they will not only spare you a great deal of labor, but will much further the success of your labors. . . . You are not likely to see any general reformation, till you procure family reformation. Some little religion there may be, here and there; but while it is confined to single persons, and is not promoted in families, it will not prosper, nor promise much future increase.[6]

When fathers fulfill their duties in their families, the role of the church leader is lightened, and the success of the leader's efforts multiplies. I love my ministry in a family-integrated church. I spend the majority of my time shepherding men and their families instead of oiling the organizational machinery. It is a real joy to see men shepherd families and hear testimonies of how God is working in them. I see lives transformed, and I know that these transformations will touch future generations. I actually have more time to spend with my own family than ever before, allowing me to live an authentic life before my flock.

## Commitment to Biblical Leadership

Family-integrated congregations are committed to biblically qualified leadership. Unfortunately, many congregations select pastors or elders on the basis of preaching or administrative skills. Little attention is given to how well the man shepherds his own family or how his family supports him in his ministry.

In my first pastorate, I followed a gifted evangelist whose teenaged sons had a reputation for spending time in jail. After he left this church, he became pastor of the largest church in the

6. R. Baxter, *The Reformed Pastor,* 93: books.google.com.

association. Obviously, this man's management and discipleship in his own household was not an issue for the pulpit committee! Yet Scripture clearly teaches that pastors must be more than great orators or skilled administrators; they must shepherd their families in ways that glorify God.

The apostle Paul exhorted members of the Philippian church to imitate him (Phil 4:9). Every church leader must provide an example that his people can imitate. That is why, according to texts such as 1 Timothy 3 and Titus 1, elders or pastors must possess two skills in addition to issues of character: the ability to teach and the ability to manage their households well (1 Tim 3:4; Titus 1:6).

The lack of qualified church leaders who manage their households well is one result of our failure in training men to lead in their homes. Home is the ideal training ground for church leadership. A church that sees reformation in families will be a church where biblically qualified pastors shepherd the congregation.

## How Family-Integrated Ministry Can Solve the Current Crisis in the Church

The church in the United States of America is facing a monumental crisis when it comes to our youth. A large part of the problem is that the church and the home are no longer the primary influences in teenagers' lives. Other more powerful forces have gained control. The largest study of teen spirituality to date was conducted by Christian Smith and a team of researchers from the University of North Carolina in Chapel Hill. Here's what Smith found in this study:

> Our research suggests that religious congregations are losing out to school and the media for the time and attention of youth. When it comes to the formation of the lives of youth, viewed sociologically, faith communities typically get a very small seat at the end of the table for a very limited period of time. The youth formation table is dominated structurally by more powerful and vocal actors. . . . Most teens know

details about television characters and pop stars, but many are quite vague about Moses and Jesus. Most youth are well versed about the dangers of drunk driving, AIDS, and drugs, but many haven't a clue about their own tradition's core ideas. Many parents also clearly prioritize homework and sports over church or youth group attendance.[7]

For most Christian teens, faith in Jesus Christ is not a vital part of their lives. Quoting Christian Smith again:

Religion seems to become rather compartmentalized and backgrounded in the lives and experiences of most U.S. teenagers. This is not surprising. It simply reflects the fact that there is very little built-in religious content or connection in the structure of most U. S. adolescents' daily schedules and routines. Most U.S. teenagers' lives are dominated by school and homework.[8]

Schools, media, and peers are the "disciplers" of America's children—discipling them in secular humanism and vague, self-centered spirituality that has nothing to do with the gospel of Jesus Christ. It is no wonder then that, once teens are no longer under their parents' direct authority, they drop their commitments like useless baggage.

The family-integrated church and family discipleship offer answers to the current crisis. Church and family alike stand in desperate need of reformation. As the church is reformed and as fathers embrace their responsibility to disciple their families as part of the fabric of their daily lives, we will glimpse a rising generation of Christian young men and women carrying the torch of the gospel to their generation.

## The Biblical and Historical Case for Family-Integrated Ministry

What does Scripture have to say about family-integrated ministry? Fathers were responsible to train their families in

---

7. C. Smith with M. Denton, *Soul Searching* (New York: Oxford University, 2005), 270.

8. Ibid., 130–31.

God's ways, families worshiped God together, and family integration was normative in communities of faith.

### Fathers Trained Their Families

From the earliest moments of human history, God gave fathers the responsibility to lead their homes to accomplish God's purposes. In Gen 18:19, the Lord said this about Abraham: "I have chosen him so that he will command his children and his house after him to keep the way of the LORD by doing what is right and just. This is how the LORD will fulfill to Abraham what He promised him."

In the opening verses of Deuteronomy 6, God commanded the men of Israel through Moses to impress the Lord's commands on their children's hearts. They were to do this as they spent their lives together, day by day. For them to occupy Canaan successfully, fathers would have to train their children to obey God's commands. If they did not impress these commands on their children, the Lord vowed to remove their inheritance from them.

Psalm 78 makes much the same point. Here, fathers receive clear instructions to teach their children to obey the Lord's commands. The motivation was so that those not yet born would know God's ways. And God did not change these expectations in the New Testament. In Eph 6:4 and Col 3:23, Paul made clear that fathers were responsible to train their children in the ways of the Lord.

### Age Integration Was Normative

Never in Scripture do we find an example of systematic age segregation in temple, synagogue, or church. In fact, we find the opposite. Children were integrated in the gathered assembly of God's people!

> Gather the people—men, women, children, and foreigners living within your gates—so that they may listen and learn to fear the LORD your God and be careful to follow all the words of this law. (Deut 31:12)

While Ezra prayed and confessed, weeping and falling face-down before the house of God, an extremely large assembly of Israelite men, women, and children gathered around him. (Ezra 10:1)

The apostle Paul expected the children to be present in the assembly of the saints. He directly addressed children in three verses of his letter to the Ephesians (6:1–3). He addressed children again in his letter to the Colossians (3:20). In first-century churches the presence of children in the church assembly was assumed.

## Families Worshiped Together

From the very beginning, families had the privilege and obligation to worship the Creator. It appears that worship at altars was a family event. Immediately after the flood, Noah and his family left the ark to build an altar to worship the Lord (Gen 8:16–20). In Genesis 22, God commanded Abraham to sacrifice his only son Isaac. As Isaac watched his father preparing the altar, he asked, "The fire and the wood are here, but where is the lamb for the burnt offering?" Clearly, this wasn't the first time Isaac had participated with his father in worship at an altar.

Thousands of years later, Jonathan Edwards had this to say about a fathers' divine obligation for times of family worship:

> Let me now therefore, once more, before I finally cease to speak to this congregation, repeat, and earnestly press the counsel which I have often urged on the heads of families, while I was their pastor, to great painfulness in teaching, warning, and directing their children; bringing them up in the training and admonition of the Lord; beginning early, where there is yet opportunity, and maintaining constant diligence in all labours of this kind.[9]

Presbyterian minister James Alexander lamented the decline of family worship in the mid-1800s:

> Our church cannot compare with that of the seventeenth century in this regard. Along with Sabbath-Observance, and

9. J. Marcellino, *Rediscovering the Lost Treasure of Family Worship* (Laurel, Miss.: Audobon, 1996), iv.

catechizing of children, Family-Worship has lost ground. There are many heads of families, communicants in our churches, and some ruling elders and deacons, who maintain no stated daily service of God in their dwellings.[10]

As we look at the condition of the twenty-first century church, it's clear that James Alexander was right to be concerned. Throughout much of church history, fathers trained their families, age integration was normative in the churches, and families practiced worship in their homes. Today these vital practices have nearly been lost, and with the loss there has also been a loss of spiritual vitality and maturity among our young adults.

## Family-Integrated Ministry—Frequently Asked Questions

Family-integrated churches are uncommon in contemporary church culture. Conditioned by age-segregated structures, people often have a difficult time fitting family-integrated ministry into their preconceived notions of what church and worship is. That is probably why we field a steady barrage of telephone calls and e-mails from church leaders and church members, most of whom are simply curious about our church. They wonder how we do worship, small groups, child training, equipping of fathers, evangelism, missions—you name it. Nearly every week, visitors come to see what a family-integrated congregation looks like. We have even organized times for curious visitors, once each quarter, in an attempt to meet this need. Still, we continue to have visitors dropping in each week to see what our church is all about.

### Misconceptions about Family-Integrated Church

One challenge we face is overcoming people's preconceived expectations. After all, most church members have now been trained for at least a couple of generations that age segregation is the *only* way to do church.

Some people confuse "family-integrated ministry" with "family-friendly" or "family-based ministry." For many church

---

10. J. Alexander, *Thoughts on Family Worship* (Morgan, Penn.: Soli Deo Gloria, 1990), 1–2.

members, that conjures up visions of a congregation where families can find a full schedule of events for everyone of every age. Some of these church members anticipate being treated like a consumer in a congregation that focuses all of its efforts on meeting their felt needs. That, however, is not what is found in a family-integrated church!

Others are looking for an enclave where they can hide with other, similar families, focusing on their families and never seeking to reach beyond their homes. Such persons are quite surprised when they discover that our mission is to equip them to reach unbelievers with the truth of the gospel.

When discovering we have no age-graded classes for children, a few people assume that family-integrated churches neglect children's spiritual training. Nothing could be further from the truth. When explaining things to these people, we say that the primary context for children's discipleship is simply changing locations: It's shifting from one hour each week in a Sunday school class to everyday discipleship and regular family worship at home. Who better to provide that teaching than the children's parents who know them best? And what better context than the home, where the events of each day are rich with opportunities for teaching, correcting, and applying biblical truth?

Sometimes family-integrated churches are mistakenly grouped with fellowships of families gathering on Sundays to do church on their own. In such gatherings fathers might take turns bringing devotions for the group each week, followed by a fellowship meal. Such fellowships typically have little or no desire to proclaim Christ in their communities. Sometimes these insulated home groups stay together for years. Yet this sort of fellowship is *not* a family-integrated church because they lack the leadership, structure, discipline, and mission of a New Testament congregation.

### What About Singles?

Once in a while people assume that *family-integrated* means that only traditional families should apply here. Some of these persons may even assume that every sermon addresses family relationships and that every Bible study teaches about the family. That is not what happens in family-integrated congregations, though. *The family is not the church, and the church is not the family.* Both institutions work together within clearly defined jurisdictional lines to bless each other and to expand Christ's kingdom.

This false assumption that traditional families are our sole interest leads some people to ask, "What do you do with singles?" Our immediate, albeit lighthearted, response is, "We eat them!" In truth, we view every single as a valuable component of Christ's body. In chapter 7 of his first letter to the Corinthians, Paul emphasized the importance of singles in the body of Christ. Singles, including not only never-marrieds but also single parents, need to hear the whole counsel of God. All Scripture speaks to all people about all issues, and God has called the whole church to be involved in calling members to embrace the whole counsel of God. Why, then, would we want to isolate singles in a singles group? Such a practice assumes that the primary place where singles and single moms will feel comfortable is with people like themselves. Yet singles need interaction with older saints who have traveled further down the road to maturity.

Single mothers need interaction with married mothers; they need the watchcare of deacons to ensure that their families receive protection and provision; their sons need relationships with men whose lives model biblical manhood. The last thing a single mom needs is to be relegated to a Sunday school class for single parents. Even singles who desire marriage should not spend all their time with other singles. They need married men and women to provide them with godly counsel as they navigate the uncharted waters of courtship and marriage.

In our family-integrated congregation, a growing number of single men and women have joined our fellowship. They enjoy the solid biblical teaching as well as the variety of relationships that family-integrated ministry offers. Plus, the single men particularly enjoy the home-cooked food they find each week at our fellowship meals!

### Are Family-Integrated Churches Evangelistic?

One final false preconception about family-integrated churches is that they are not evangelistic. This is simply false. It is possible that when these critics think of evangelism, they think of a church program. And since we have no program listed in the bulletin, maybe they assume that we don't do evangelism. Yet the evangelistic nature of a church is not found in a church's structure; it's found in whether the people are obedient to the Great Commission. An evangelistic church is one whose leadership proclaims Christ to all people and equips members to do the same.

The home is one effective place to invite unbelievers and to witness to them. Yet family-integrated churches do not limit evangelism to homes. Every church member is responsible to share the message of Jesus Christ with lost friends and neighbors throughout the week.

Family-integrated churches can and do actively engage in evangelism. In addition to sharing the gospel throughout the week in their homes and at work, men from our church share a witness each week on the streets of Houston. Other church members witness as they serve in a pregnancy help center, located across the street from one of the largest abortion clinics in the United States. Still others intentionally invite unbelievers into their homes to share not only Christian hospitality but also the good news of Jesus Christ.

## Challenges to Transitioning Churches to a Family-Integrated Model

When churches pursue radically different paradigms, the challenge is overcoming conditioning absorbed while working in other church frameworks. As the leader in a family-integrated church, you cannot simply cut and paste what you did in previous ministry contexts! You are forced to rethink every method you have used in the past, not only in children's ministry and youth ministry but also in men's ministry, women's ministry, worship, preaching, hospitality, evangelism, leadership, church government, and deacon ministry.

### Rebuilding Relationships Broken by Age Segregation

It isn't just church leadership that's challenged, though. People who come to your church are also likely to face some challenges. Some families whose youth have been in age-segregated ministries sometimes struggle to adjust to family-integrated ministry. In some cases a young person is so tightly connected to a youth group that he or she is more committed to that youth group than their own family. That's one of the sad results of age-segregated ministry—parents have lost their children's hearts, and we face the challenge of trying to help them to rebuild those relationships.

Family integration can help to rebuild relationships, but this rebuilding also requires repentance on the part of parents before their children. It requires intense redirection of the parents' affections and priorities toward their children. And yet we still have families in our church who are waiting to regain their children's hearts. Many families do, however, come to our church from age-segregated congregations, and their children couldn't be happier. The transition really depends on the relationship between the parents and children.

### Training Husbands and Wives in Their God-Ordained Roles

Men especially must be retrained in family-integrated churches. Many men must move from merely bringing their families to church to embracing their God-ordained role as their families' spiritual shepherd and mentor. Some men have no desire to fulfill God's expectation. If so, the family-integrated church is not for them. It is biblical for men to serve as spiritual mentors for their families, and a family-integrated church will lovingly but firmly hold men accountable to fulfill this role.

For men who are willing to embrace this calling, we provide the encouragement and equipping they need to succeed. Men who are willing quickly discover they are not alone; other men are standing with them and supporting them on their journey toward biblical manhood.

Wives may have to make some adjustments, too. Faced with passive husbands, many women have assumed the role of spiritual leader in their homes. Their attitude has been, "If I don't take charge of spiritual growth in our home, it won't get done!" For these wives it is a challenge to relinquish control of their families and to embrace their biblical role as complementary helpers for their husbands. Mature women in a family-integrated church are invaluable in providing these struggling women with hope, encouragement, and biblical counsel.

## Training Children for Family Integration

Children also must adjust. In many current church structures, there is no need for parents to train their children to sit still and to pay attention. Why should they, when nursery and children's church are so readily available? Yet it is the parents' biblical responsibility to train their children well (Prov 13:24; 22:6,15; 23:13; 29:15).

If parents have neglected their children's training, family-integrated church can be a bit unsettling at first. Yet these parents also experience a sense of hope as they sit in our services and watch children sit still for two hours! For parents who have neglected the training of their children, we provide books, an occasional small group, and rods—yes, we provide rods to assist in disciplining children! These rods are flexible, about eight inches long, an inch and a half wide, and only one-eighth of an inch thick. These are *not* instruments that could be used to injure a child in any way. To the contrary, they're specifically constructed to cause some pain but never to facilitate any form of child abuse. They fit easily in a purse or pocket to make it easy for parents to be consistent in child training.

One family visited our church with three small boys—a three-year-old and two-year-old twins. The children weren't accustomed to remaining in the church service. At first, the parents were taken aback by the fact that we had no nursery. Nonetheless, the father found a child-training book and a rod. A few weeks later his boys were a joy to see in worship, and it *is* a joy to watch toddlers worshiping with their families. Every once in a while, one can even hear an "amen" from one of these little guys or hear a tiny girl whisper, "Daddy, that's my favorite song!" The children are learning to honor their parents and to worship God with the congregation.

Another challenge in family-integrated churches is reaching parents whose children are in public school. Most of our families educate their children at home. This is probably because home educators and family integrators share many of the same values. We do *not*, however, target homeschool families; they seek us out! We have reached some public-school families; we long to reach more. Our desire is to see all sorts of people, not only intact families and homeschoolers but also public school families, Christian school families, single parents, shattered families, never marrieds—all transformed by God's grace.

## Family Integration and the Measurement of Success

How can the success of a family-integrated church be measured? Unfortunately, pragmatism rules in our culture and in many of our churches. As a result, success is often measured by size and budget rather than faithfulness. In his book *The Courage to Be Protestant,* David Wells questions the pragmatic measures of success in many market-driven churches:

> Can we argue with success? I believe that we can. More than that, in this case, I believe that we must, that we should. What we have here are churches reconfigured around evangelism that abandon much of the fabric of biblical faith to succeed. They have taken a part of that faith, modified it in deference to consumer impulse, and then made of that part all that there is to Christian faith. Here is a methodology for success that can succeed with very little truth; indeed, its success seems to depend on not showing much truth.[11]

---

11. D. Wells, *The Courage to Be Protestant* (Grand Rapids, Mich.: Eerdmans, 2008), 51.

The temptation to measure success "with very little truth" is greater than any of us would care to admit. It is difficult *not* to measure success by budgets and numbers when salaries and positions depend on maintaining the organization. "Not losing members" can quickly become the highest priority in a congregation. One of my friends was discussing family integration with a senior pastor who gave this reply: "The theology [of family integration and family discipleship] sounds right, but the application has to be wrong because our people can't do it and it would make our church shrink." This man was an ecclesiological pragmatist. He had defined not only right success but also right theology according to what seemed to work from a human perspective.

Before homes and churches can ever experience spiritual reformation, biblical standards for success must replace ecclesiological pragmatism. It is so easy to wear cultural lenses and to read culturally accepted practices into Holy Scripture. That's also why it's so important to step outside of our culture by reading the works of saints who lived in other times and places.

In evaluating the success of a family-integrated church, it is necessary to ask questions such as these: Does this structure reflect the ideal structure of New Testament churches? Does the church's leadership meet the qualifications that are spelled out in the Bible? Are the structures of leadership biblical? Is the preaching faithful to the text of Scripture? Are men leading their families? Are parents discipling their children? Are wives helping and submitting to their husbands? Are children obeying the fifth commandment? Are there ministries of intergenerational discipleship that reflect the sound teaching principles of Titus 2:1–8? Do we practice hospitality toward one another and toward the world? Are we engaging in biblical evangelism?

A church is successful only to the degree that it lines up with Scripture in these areas. To the degree that we lead God's church biblically, we will experience his blessing, not necessarily in buildings and money but in churches that closely resemble what Jesus and the apostles expected churches to look like.

The family-integrated model is the best approach to family ministry because such a model calls men to the sacred vocation of family discipleship. Family integration removes the age-segregating structures that work against intergenerational discipleship. Integration returns time to families, so that families can be families—living, learning, working, ministering, worshiping, and playing together. The family-integrated model of ministry allows pastors in the body of Christ the time to shepherd their flock and their family for the glory of God.

# CHAPTER 6

# Responses to Paul Renfro
## Family-Integrated Ministry

### Response by Brandon Shields

As I was reading Paul Renfro's description of family-integrated ministry, I was encouraged by the heartfelt love, fellowship, and family interaction that take place in this particular congregation of believers. With Renfro, I support teenagers interacting with older believers and families enjoying intimate times together as part of the gathered community of faith. Such practices are commendable.

At the same time many aspects of the family-integrated perspective trouble me. They trouble me because I believe they blunt the local church's efforts to penetrate youth culture with the gospel of Jesus Christ. There are three specific points where I must question whether family integration represents the best approach to family ministry: First, family-integrated congregations describe the church primarily as a "family of families" when actually the church is not a "family of families" but the family of God. Second, family-integrated churches are structured in such a way that public-school families are less likely to be reached for Christ. And third, although they claim to be completely integrated, even so-called family-integrated churches selectively segregate members.

## The Church Is Not Primarily a "Family of Families"

According to Voddie Baucham, proponents of family-integrated ministry "see the church as a family of families."[1] When using the term "family of families," family-integrated ministers seem to imply that the family serves as the primary hub for evangelism and discipleship in the church. Viewed in this way, a rightly ordered church is a collection of family units both independently and interdependently fulfilling the biblical mandates that God has given to the church. Such a perspective seems to be grounded in an Old Testament patriarchal view of the covenant community, where physical heritage validated membership in the visible Israelite community.

This perspective on the church was clear throughout Paul Renfro's chapter. Prayer guides enlisting support for families, the church holding fathers accountable for leading family worship in their homes, fathers gathering their families for prayer before the Lord's Supper, small groups involving entire families, and so on. In every instance the emphasis is placed on participation as a *biological family unit* or *nuclear family*, underscoring this "family of families" type of ecclesiology.

The church is not, however, primarily a family of families! I find it curious that the family-integrated church, with its heavy emphasis on a regulative view of Scripture, summarizes its ecclesiology in a way that is foreign to Scripture. The biblical depiction of the church is far broader and far more diverse than the perspective highlighted in family-integrated churches. The New Testament church is not a family of families but *the family of God* (1 Cor 12; Rom 12; 1 Pet. 4:17; 1 Tim 3:15). The authors of the New Testament employed familial language that moved beyond biological bloodlines to include any individual who would place his or her faith in the Lord Jesus Christ. Inclusion among the people of God had nothing to do with birthright in a nuclear family and everything to do with adoption into the family of God (Eph 1:4–6; Gal 4:1–7; Rom 8).

Jesus himself articulates this transfamilial perspective several times in the Gospels. Consider these words from the lips

---

1. Baucham, *Family Driven Faith*, 191–95.

of Jesus: "Whoever does the will of God is My brother and sister and mother" (Mark 3:33–35). Jesus also declared, "Don't assume that I came to bring peace on the earth. I did not come to bring peace, but a sword. For I came to turn a man against his father, a daughter against her mother, . . . a man's enemies will be the members of his household" (Matt 10:34–36). In essence, Jesus was saying that a believer's spiritual family is a permanent institution consisting of those who have submitted their hearts to the rule of Jesus Christ. This new reality may or may not include the believer's family of origin, and many times it does not.

Family-integrated congregations recast the church's mission in a way that has broad implications for ministry. Practically speaking, family-integrated churches replace a primary emphasis on conversion and discipleship of lost persons with a primary focus on evangelism and training in the context of family. Such a strategy becomes problematic when it is elevated to a place of primacy in the church's economy. After all, the nuclear family is *not* God's primary mechanism for accomplishing the Great Commission mandate of evangelism and discipleship; rather, the local church clearly bears this responsibility (1 Cor 12; Eph 4:11–13).

Of course, fulfilling this mandate isn't a solo mission. The church *is* called to partner with families, where they exist, to fulfill the mission of Jesus in the world. And, admittedly, as fathers love their wives and disciple their children, they play an essential part in the mission of God (Ps 127; Col 3.; Eph 6). Yet, when a church restructures itself to function as a "family of families," can members really say they are fully focused on the church's global task of evangelism and discipleship?

## Public-School Families Are Not Being Adequately Reached

The family-integrated church model is passionate about reaching the lost, but even so there is a tendency to attract nearly exclusively intact, homeschooling Christian families. Why do these families gravitate toward family-integrated churches? In part, there is simply the sociological reality that people tend to feel more comfortable with people like themselves.

I do, however, see a much stronger catalyst driving these congregants toward family-integrated churches. For some families, homeschooling enables them to escape the perceived corruption of the public school system, effectively guarding their children from negative influences. Unfortunately for the growth of family-integrated churches, homeschooling families represent only the tiniest slice of American households. Consider these statistics:

- In 2007, nearly fifty-six million total students attended some form of elementary or secondary schooling in the United States.
- Of these 55.8 million students, 49.6 million were enrolled in the public education system.
- A 2003 study estimated that there were 1.1 million home-educated students;[2] the current population of home-schooled students stands, at most, around two million.[3]

This means that out of nearly fifty-six million elementary and secondary students, the family-integrated movement works primarily with *less than 2 percent of the student population*! And what about the 3.7 million people who *work* in the public school system?

The fact is that the vast majority of Americans—Christians and non-Christians—send their children to public schools. Yet family-integrated churches do not seem to be passionate about or properly positioned for effecting Christ-centered change in the lives of nearly fifty million public-school students and their families. The public schools—and, specifically, the youth culture found there—are the largest mission field in America. How can family-integrated churches realistically answer God's call to this mission field?

## Every Church Segregates

Proponents of family-integrated ministry argue passionately against any systematic "age segregation." Yet, at several points

---

2. Digest of Education Statistics: 2007. Accessed from nces.ed.gov/programs/digest/d07/.

3. National Home Education Research Institute, *Research Facts on Home Schooling*: www.nheri.org/Research-Facts-on-Home-Schooling.html.

throughout the chapter, Paul Renfro presented examples that were implicitly inconsistent with this perspective.

In his discussion of evangelism, for example, he mentioned how the men of the church witness in the streets of Houston. Unless these men are bringing their wives, teenagers, younger children, and infants with them, this represents age and gender segregation. The same might be said for the monthly men's breakfast and perhaps the opportunities for volunteering at the local pregnancy center. And what about the children charged with helping to set up multimedia and the women and girls who prepare the fellowship meal? Each of these patterns in congregational life represents some form of age or gender segmentation for specific tasks.

By necessity, every church chooses some degree of segregation in its organization. Family-integrated churches have decided to refuse to segregate the generations for worship and small groups. Yet they are willing to segregate for the purpose of encouraging fathers and young men. Family-based churches extend this same pattern to Sunday morning small groups and sometimes to worship celebrations in order to promote age-appropriate evangelism, fellowship, and instruction. Why? Because it is virtually impossible to engage in targeted learning without some form of age-organized instruction. If segmentation by age or gender is indeed the root cause of family fragmentation and high church dropout rates among young adults, *any* system or activity that excludes family members because of their age or gender comes up short.

## A Fine Approach—for a Few People

I appreciated the concern for families that family-integrated churches aptly demonstrate; I particularly appreciated Paul Renfro's emphasis on the importance of encouraging fathers. An epidemic of weak male leadership seems to be present in churches of every size and every denomination. The family-integrated approach tackles this problem with seriousness and intensity. Yet I have profound concerns with both the lack of a missional posture

toward public-school families and with the false dichotomy between age-organized ministries and biblical discipleship.

Family-integrated ministry is *one way* to approach family
ministry. It appeals to certain kinds of people in specific circumstances. Yet the difficulties I have mentioned will prevent most
evangelical churches from successfully implementing ministry
based on a family-integrated approach.

## Response by Jay Strother

I deeply appreciate how family-integrated churches courageously seek to recover the biblical connection between families and the faith community. The family-integrated church is a
model that is, first of all, striking in its *clarity*. In an era wherein
so many congregations struggle with their ecclesiological identity, family-integrated churches know their calling, and they are
unashamed in that mission. More churches need to understand
and to pursue whatever unique mission God has set before them
in their community. There's an old saying: "If you aim at nothing, you will hit it every time." Family-integrated churches do
not seem to struggle with this issue of a "target" audience; for
them, the target is clearly the family, and they appeal to this target with passion and skill.

Second, family-integrated church represents "simple
church" at its finest. Too many midsized and larger evangelical churches offer an overwhelming variety of opportunities,
aiming at every conceivable age group or interest group. Such
wide-ranging choices are puzzling to typical churchgoers, and
they are utterly mystifying for newcomers. The leaders of these
churches are often guilty of adding new programs without having the courage to eliminate existing programs, leaving everyone
competing for leadership, space, resources, and attention. The
family-integrated model cuts through this clutter with a simple
plan: family worship on Sundays and family discipleship groups
in homes during the week. As Thom Rainer and Eric Geiger note,
"Churches have become cluttered. So cluttered that people have
a difficult time encountering the simple and powerful message

of Jesus Christ. So cluttered that many people are busy *doing* church instead of *being* the church."[4] The family-integrated approach places less emphasis on church programs and more emphasis on the home—a much-needed course correction for most congregations.

As a church leader who has seen firsthand the devastating effects of absent or spiritually disconnected fathers, I am also moved when I see how the family-integrated church challenges men to be spiritual leaders. In the book *Why Men Hate Going to Church,* David Murrow notes that when a *mother* comes to faith in Christ, the rest of her family follows 17 percent of the time; however, when the *father* comes to faith, the family joins him 93 percent of the time. In other words, as men go, so goes the church.[5] The family-integrated church calls men to become full participants in the mission of leading their homes.

## Questions for the Family-Integrated Model

Despite the strengths of this model, several honest questions must be raised about family-integrated ministry. My first question is simply this: How would you transition the typical North American church into this model of ministry? For all of its clarity and simplicity, it appears that it would be extremely difficult to effect such a transition. Is there any space for incrementalism in the transition? I agree with Paul Renfro that our motivation should never be only "not to lose members." At the same time it is not "ecclesiological pragmatism" to move your church slowly and consistently toward a more biblical view of the family in a way that avoids strife and division. That's simply wise leadership. It might be effective to *plant* family-integrated churches. Yet it doesn't seem that a smooth transition to this model would be feasible for tens of thousands of American churches desperately seeking ways to reconnect the church and home.

Here is the second question that I would raise: "How do family-integrated churches plan to reach nontraditional families and help these families understand themselves as full participants in the body of Christ?" Approximately three out of every

---

4. T. Rainer and E. Geiger. *Simple Church* (Nashville, Tenn.: B&H, 2007), 19.
5. D. Murrow, *Why Men Hate Going to Church* (Nashville, Tenn.: Nelson, 2005), 47.

ten children in the United States are being raised in single-parent homes.[6] In 2006, around 35 percent of all births were to women who were separated, widowed, divorced, or never married. Furthermore, more than ninety million American adults are unmarried. The structure of a family-integrated church could discourage many singles and nontraditional families from full participation in their community of faith. What happens with the teenager whose parents are spiritually or physically absent? If Bible studies take place in homes led by fathers, what learning opportunities are provided for single mothers in need of guidance from more mature women? Could it be that family-integrated churches so heavily emphasize traditional family structures that they subtly give nontraditional families the impression they are second-class citizens in God's kingdom? Such an impression would oppose the very testimony of Scripture, wherein God commands his people to provide special care for orphans and widows (Ps 68:5; Jas 1:27).

Another question that this family-integrated church model compels me to ask is, "How do you equip children and youth to engage contemporary culture with their faith?" If parents shelter their children and teenagers from all competing worldviews, their children may be ill equipped to make wise decisions as adults. In addition, if children and youth do not learn to relate constructively to their peers, they are less capable of sharing the gospel with these peers. Although family-integrated ministry is not necessarily to blame for such failures, family-integrated church could create an environment promoting unhealthy sheltering of children and youth.

### Challenging Some Family-Integrated Assumptions

There also seem to be a few faulty assumptions in Paul Renfro's chapter when it comes to churches with age-organized ministries. In the first place he seems to link age-organized ministry with the necessity of spending 90 percent of one's time focused on administrative tasks. Perhaps this *does* occur in some churches,

---

6. www.census.gov/Press-Release/www/releases/archives/facts_for_features_special_editions/012633.html and single-parenting.families.com/blog/just-how-many-single-parents-are-there.

but it certainly hasn't been the case in my ministry. Our ministry strives to follow an "80/20 rule": spend 80 percent of the time engaging in ministry and 20 percent of the time administrating. If administrative tasks consume more than 20 percent of a staff member's time, it is our responsibility to reprioritize our schedule to eliminate programs or events that take too much time or to delegate some tasks to others (Exod 18; Acts 6:1–7). Simply because a church is age organized does not inevitably mean the church's ministers spend the majority of their time "oiling the machinery." In family-equipping churches, biblical practices of leadership and time management provide us with time to exercise our spiritual gifts, to engage in ministry, and to nurture significant relationships without neglecting the discipleship of families.

The second faulty point that I want to challenge has to do with "the myth of adolescence." I recognize, with proponents of family integration, that adolescence—as it is perceived and practiced in our culture—*is* a recent phenomenon. Yet, at this particular point in history, adolescence is also a societal actuality that is probably not going to fade away anytime soon. Adolescence is a recent social construction, but this social construction is also a cultural reality. Millions of adolescents in the United States desperately need to experience the gospel of Jesus Christ in ways they can understand within their cultural contexts.

Paul Renfro points out that placing adolescent peers together can perpetuate immaturity. I have a lifetime of ministry experience to back him up on this point. (A group of guys collaborating in a cabin to determine the precise flammability of hand sanitizer comes to mind.) At the same time, I've also seen students raised in church-home partnerships who were well equipped not only to reach other traditional families but also to present the gospel message to lost peers from shattered homes.

Age-organized ministries can be expressions of missional zeal for unbelieving people around us. I am so glad that this family-integrated congregation prays weekly for unreached people groups, but I wonder if they remember that unbelieving teenagers in North America make up one of the most significant people groups on the planet? How will family-integrated congregations reach youth whose families remain unchurched?

Finally, I question the notion that parents whose children developed strong relationships in youth groups have "lost their children's hearts." Lost their hearts to *whom*? If a student has developed relationships with other caring adults who have committed themselves to speaking God's truth into this student's life, I have difficulty describing this in terms of "losing their children's hearts." No set of parents possesses all wisdom or every spiritual gift. If parents have lost their children's hearts to the culture or to unbiblical worldviews, that's another issue; but to suggest that age-organized ministries, in themselves, cause disconnection between parents and children is an overstatement. The typical church-based student ministry teaches a youth for forty or so hours each year; parents have more than three thousand hours per year to disciple their child. Can the investment of one or two hours each week in Bible study with a supportive peer group, led by a spiritually mature adult, truly cause parents to "lose their child's heart"?

Like family-integrated churches, family-equipping churches focus on biblical standards guiding every aspect of congregational life. We worship together intergenerationally, with only the tiniest of our toddlers and infants spending time in preschool ministry. We train fathers to become spiritual leaders in their homes. We establish mentoring relationships that enact Titus 2:1–8 at every level of congregational life. We commit ourselves to evangelism and discipleship in and through the home. We call only church leaders who meet the biblical qualifications of managing their homes in a godly way.

In reality, the only glaring difference between the family-equipping model and the family-integrated approach is that we have chosen to maintain some age-organized ministries. I contend that the family-equipping church accomplishes virtually the same goals as the family-integrated congregation without the total elimination of age-organized ministry. Martin Luther once described a well-meaning peasant who "climbed up one side of the horse only to fall off the other." The point that the Reformer was making is that, if we are not careful, we can simply move from one extreme to another. The same might be said about our attempts to recognize the family as the primary context for discipleship. Proponents of family-integrated ministry rightly point out that many age-organized congregations are failing to bring families together. Yet I fear that they may have—with the best of intentions—climbed up one side of the horse only to take a tumble off the other.

# Why Family Integration Still Works

### Paul Renfro

The family-integrated church represents a complete paradigm shift, drawing the people of God back to a more biblical and historical model of ministry. In this response I will draw attention to seven points at which proponents of other perspectives seem to misunderstand how family-integrated ministry functions.

### Misunderstanding 1: What We Mean by "Family of Families"

When we describe the church as a "family of families," we are addressing *the structure of the church* and not *the nature of the church*. God created the family as the primary training ground for children. Cultural deterioration and family disintegration do not and cannot change that fact. Proponents of family integration are *not* using the term "family of families" to discuss *the nature of the church*. The church is the body of "saints" or "called out ones." Only those who have embraced Christ alone for salvation are part of the church. That is the church's essential nature. Our discussion and our use of the term "family of families" focuses on *how to structure the church to facilitate family discipleship*, not on how Christians ought to view the nature of the church.

To hear some quote the words of Jesus in Matthew 10:34–37, you would think that part of the Lord's primary mission was to tear families apart. Yet this text has to do with the breaking of family relationships that can occur when some family members embrace the gospel while others do not. Such straining of relationships is as ancient as the first family. (Remember Cain and Abel?) Nonetheless, throughout history, God's plan has been to use families to convey His truth to future generations. Our discussions have been about finding biblical balance, allowing the church and the family to fulfill their God-given roles.

### Misunderstanding 2: Does Family Discipleship Distract from World Evangelism?

Another primary misperception that persists in Brandon's response is that since family-integrated churches focus on family evangelism and discipleship, this means that family integrationists fail to focus on world evangelization. Nothing could be further from the truth.

Age-segregated churches have, for the most part, focused primarily on evangelism of young people while neglecting discipleship, especially family discipleship. The result has been the tragic loss of many youth, the very people who should have evangelized the next generation.

In the family-integrated church, it is not a question of either/or, but both/and—both family discipleship *and* world evangelism. The mandates of Scripture call believers to evangelize and disciple their children precisely so they can evangelize the world with the help and the testimony of their faithful children. How compelling is a religion that cannot keep its own children? There is no greater joy than proclaiming the gospel alongside our children, and there is no greater heartache than knowing we have lost our own children to the world.

## Misunderstanding 3: Do Family-Integrated Churches Target Intact Families?

In our particular family-integrated congregation, the church's mission statement is "proclaiming the supremacy of Christ to all men with a view toward biblical conversion and comprehensive discipleship." Nothing in this statement suggests that intact families are our congregation's primary target. Yet proponents of other ministry models seem to suggest that family-integrated churches reach only intact families and that by organizing ministries according to certain age groupings, family-based and family-equipping churches can reach more people.

This idea is based on a couple of false assumptions: The first false assumption is that the current age-segregated model has actually been successful. The fact is that age-segregated structures have consistently failed to reach and to retain youth and children. Alvin Reid addresses the failure of age-segregated youth ministry in his book *Raising the Bar:*

> The largest rise in full-time youth ministers in history has been accompanied by the biggest decline in youth evangelism effectiveness. . . . For the past three decades, . . . youth ministry has exploded across America, accompanied by a rise in the number of degrees in youth ministry granted by colleges and seminaries, an abundance of books and other resources, and a network of cottage industries devoted solely to youth ministry. Yet these same three decades have failed to produce a generation of young people who graduate from high school or leave youth groups ready to change the world for Christ.[7]

Despite thirty years of exponential increases in staffing and resources, age-segregated ministry has failed in its goal to reach a generation of youth. If age-segregated ministry *had* been successful, youth culture would not be "the largest mission field in America"!

---

7. A. Reid, *Raising the Bar: Ministry to Youth in the New Millennium* (Grand Rapids, Mich.: Kregel, 2004), 38.

The other false assumption is that family-integrated congregations, with so many intact families involved in their churches, cannot consistently reach singles, single-parent families, adolescents raised in the youth culture, or public-school families. Where do we get this idea that "like" can only reach "like"? While some similarities can be beneficial, the gospel is not limited by our dissimilarity to a certain audience. God called the apostle Paul—a very Jewish Pharisee—to be an apostle to the uncircumcised Gentiles. You can't get much more dissimilar than that.

What the church needs to reach the lost is *not* the relatively new concept of age segregation. What the church needs is faithful proclamation of Scripture and an authentic faith-community that strives to obey the Lord's commands, including "making disciples of all nations." Which scenario exemplifies Christ-centered unity better: a church that highlights differences by dividing families and singles into separate groupings or a church that highlights the common bond we all have in Christ by worshiping and ministering together? The church does not have to look like the culture to be effective. God made Israel a peculiar people to reach the other nations of the world. The more distinct the church is, the more powerful its message.

### Misunderstanding 4: Family-Integrated Churches and Home Education

The discussion of family-integrated church eventually gets around to the issue of educational choice. Brandon assumes that family-integrated churches "do not seem to be passionate about or properly positioned for effecting Christ-centered change in the lives of nearly fifty million public-school students and their families." But in fact, family-integrated churches are passionate about *all* people in *all* families, regardless of their educational choices.

At the same time, because of our concern for these families and because of our God-given responsibility as shepherds, we believe in speaking truth regarding the problems in present systems of public education. The problems with public schooling are not merely supposed or perceived; they are very real, resulting in widespread, systematic indoctrination of children in secular humanism. The result of speaking truth about the problems with public schooling is that many of our families choose home education.

The Nehemiah Institute has tested the worldviews of Christian students since the 1980s. In 2001, the Nehemiah Institute pointed out that if downward trends in biblical perspectives continue at the present rate among students in public schools and traditional Christian schools, the "next generation of Christian adults" will have to be labeled as "'Committed Secular Humanists with leanings toward Socialism' between the years 2014 and 2018."[8] Church leaders cannot ignore the fact that some sort of discipleship, whether positive or negative, God honoring or God denying, occurs in every educational process.[9] Now, contrast the dismal findings from the Nehemiah Institute with another study, which revealed that 94 percent of home-educated students retain the religious beliefs and practices of their parents.[10]

Jay wonders whether, "if parents shelter their children and teenagers from all competing worldviews," home-educated children can relate adequately to their peers and make wise adult decisions. In the first place, most home educators do not shelter their children from competing worldviews. In fact, they educate their older children both in a biblical worldview and in competing worldviews. Their children are not sheltered from competing perspectives but are equipped to respond biblically to false worldviews.

In the second place, exposing children to competing worldviews in public schools does not necessarily result in these students' being able to resist false perspectives. As a teacher in public school classrooms, I saw very few Christian students who were adequately prepared to deal with the worldviews they encountered in public school. Far more often I observed Christian students being influenced by their unbelieving peers. Children from Christian homes who were immersed in youth culture and

8. "Where Are We Going?": www.nehemiahinstitute.com.
9. For discussion of environmental issues in public education, as well as the issue of socialization in home education, see M. Wilder, "There's No Place like Home," in *Perspectives on Children's Education,* ed. T. Jones (Nashville, Tenn.: B&H, 2009).
10. B. Ray, *Home Educated and Now Adults* (Salem, Ore.: NHERI, 2004), 83.

indoctrinated in secular humanism often became converts of the culture, joining the majority of young adult church members who disengage from their faith by their second year in college. And why do these students leave the church? In many cases, after fourteen thousand seat-hours in public schools, they have simply lost any semblance of a biblical worldview.

Children raised with strong family discipleship are able not only to relate to their peers but also to relate to other age groups. They stand against peer pressure and proclaim the truth of Christ because they are not dependent on approval from their peers. "The one who walks with the wise will become wise," the inspired author of Proverbs observed, "but a companion of fools will suffer harm" (Prov 13:20).

Some seem to assume that church members must have children in public schools to reach public school students. But let's apply this logic further: If we desire to reach Muslim youth, does this strategy require that we place our children in Muslim schools? Do we need to put some of our children in Roman Catholic schools to reach Catholics? And what about Jewish schools? Do we enroll our children in Jewish schools so that they can be salt and light among the Jewish people? Christians must equip their children, grounding them in truth, and then launch them to be missionaries in the culture. When we send raw recruits into the battle, they do not typically end up as warriors of light; instead, they become cannon fodder for the Enemy.

In sum, yes, many parents in family-integrated churches educate their children at home but not because home-educators are our target audience. In our short existence as a church, we *have* reached public-school families, and we continue to work toward the goal of reaching more. The difference is that we reach parents first and the children naturally follow, allowing us to disciple entire families.

### Misunderstanding 5: Losing Children's Hearts?

We *are* concerned about parents losing children's hearts in age-graded contexts, but our concern is *not* about losing children's hearts to godly, caring adult mentors. Our concern has to do with losing children's hearts to their peers and to peer influences. Between typical school and church programs, age segregation places most children in our culture with their peers for inordinate amounts of time. The result in many cases is that children care more about what their peers think than about what their parents think.

## Misunderstanding 6: All Churches Segregate?

Brandon tries to make the case for age segregation by claiming that "any system or activity that excludes family members because of their age or gender comes up short" if a church embraces family integration. This represents an absolute misapprehension of family-integrated ministry. Family-integrated churches practice no formal age segregation, which means that we do not organize church ministries by age. Put another way, our ministries are intentionally intergenerational.

At no time have the primary proponents of family-integrated ministry claimed that informal groupings are inherently inappropriate. In our particular congregation, street evangelism includes primarily single men with some fathers participating from time to time with older sons. The monthly men's meeting is for all men in the church—husbands, fathers, and young men twelve and older—and is clearly multigenerational.

## Misunderstanding 7: Is Transition Unrealistic?

I appreciate how Jay admits that transitioning a congregation into a family-equipping model is slow and difficult. Undoing a generation of training in age segregation is no easy feat, especially for churches choosing to retain some age-segregated structures. We in the family-integrated movement acknowledge that many churches will not be able to make the transition to full family integration. At the same time, some movement toward family integration is possible in any congregation, and there are churches that have made a full transition.

Here are ten transitional principles to consider: (1) Lay a biblical foundation for family integration through the church's proclamation and teaching. (2) At the same time, be certain that the church's leadership models family discipleship. (3) Equip heads of households to become spiritual leaders in their homes. Provide them with simple plans for family worship, and make child training a priority if children have not yet learned to sit with their parents in worship services. (4) Encourage heads of households to evaluate their families' priorities and to prune their families' calendars, eliminating activities that have crowded out family time. (5) In times of worship, begin having children and adults worship together. (6) Reduce age-segregated events. (7) Transition small groups to age-integrated groups. (8) Transition Sunday school toward age-integration. (9) Transition ministries toward age-integration. (10) Transition mission efforts toward age-integration.

## Why the Family-Integrated Model Remains the Most Effective

We applaud the efforts of the family-based and family-equipping models. Yet age-segregated structures that remain in place in family-based and family-equipping churches make family reformation more difficult by tacitly reinforcing the false notion that professional ministers are the people primarily responsible for children's discipleship.

The beauty of the family-integrated model is that it breaks completely free from these age-segregated structures. In family-integrated churches, heads of households assume their rightful place as spiritual leaders in their homes. All family types are equipped to engage in family discipleship. Everyone worships, learns, and ministers together, while the very structure and culture of the church provide fertile soil for the sorts of relationships the apostle Paul described in Titus 2:1–8. Family-integrated churches recover the lost art of Christian hospitality, reestablishing the home as a center for ministry and evangelism. Simple calendars in family-integrated churches provide time for family discipleship and for authentic Christian community. The churches experience better pastoral care as fathers shepherd their own families and as pastors have time both to disciple their own families and to guide the body of Christ.

The family-integrated model is simple, effective, and reproducible in any cultural context, foreign or domestic. After more than a half century of age segregation, the family-integrated model may seem extreme to many people, but it is a model calling God's people to ancient patterns of community and discipleship—crucial patterns from the earliest centuries of church history.

CHAPTER 7

# Family-Based Ministry
## SEPARATED CONTEXTS, SHARED FOCUS
### Brandon Shields

*Minister to High School Students*
*Highview Baptist Church*

Family-based ministry isn't so much a fixed model of ministry as it is a ministry philosophy. The two core values undergirding this philosophy are *flexibility* and *balance*. Proponents of family-based ministry value flexibility because they know that every church culture is different and that ministry models must adapt to be effective. Family-based ministers value balance because they recognize that, even though encouraging the discipleship efforts of intact Christian families is important, most youth and children today do not enjoy the sociological luxury of an intact Christian family. Family-based ministry supports Christian families where they exist while, at the same time, aggressively and intentionally engaging non-Christian families with the transforming message of Jesus Christ.

The family-based posture resembles typical age-organized youth and children's ministries with an important twist: "We are not suggesting a radical change in programming. What we are suggesting is a fresh mindset: Parents and family are crucial to faith development in every area of a ministry's program."[1] Family-based ministry recognizes that there are no pressing rea-

---

1. J. Burns and M. DeVries, *Partnering with Parents in Youth Ministry* (Ventura, Calif.: Regal, 2003), 7.

sons for radical reorganization or restructuring of present ministry models. There is certainly no need for complete integration of age groups. What churches need to do is simply refocus existing age-appropriate groupings to partner intentionally with families in the discipleship process.

In family-based ministry, "the job of the church is to keep the priority of family at the forefront of our mission, to give families the understanding and tools they need to raise their children to continue to grow their legacy of faith."[2] As family-based pioneer Mark DeVries has noted,

> Most people confuse the starting of a family-based youth ministry with a radical change in programming. . . . But family-based youth ministry is not about what the programming looks like. It's about what you use the programming for. We try to point as much of our programming as possible in the direction of giving kids and adults excuses to interact together.[3]

DeVries refers to the process of taking current activities and turning them into family events as "exfamizing" activities. Family-based churches constantly look for opportunities to engage in exfamization.[4]

What does this mean at the level of the local church? Practically, this means that my family-based church still hosts age-graded, gender-specific small groups every Sunday morning. Many children go to Extreme Zone while their parents participate in weekend worship celebrations. There is still a weekly large-group service for youth where we preach the gospel, worship together, and hang out in the gym. There are yearly children's and youth camps as well as retreats that are organized by age, gender, or life stage. At the same time, our programs work with parents in discipling their children. This weekend the youth ministry will kick off a Sunday night ministry to dads entitled, "Becoming a Man," which combines a study on manhood with father-son

---

2. Ibid., 16.
3. M. DeVries, et al., Youth Ministry Architects Web site: www.ymarchitects.com/resources.html.
4. DeVries and Palmer, *Family-Based Youth Ministry*, rev. ed., 179–80.

competitions that provide busy dads with weekly opportunities to engage with their sons and with other dads. This spring our youth ministry will host a Joy Prom, where parents and their kids work together to throw a celebration party for young adults with Down syndrome. Our goal is to provide a platform for families to catch a vision for discipling their own teenagers.

---

### What's Distinctive about a "Family-Based Church"?

Family-based churches retain separate, age-segmented ministry structures. The difference between family-based models and typical programmatic models is that family-based churches intentionally include intergenerational and family-focused events in each ministry.

---

## Age Segregation Isn't the Problem

Despite its clear usefulness in local churches over the past fifty years, age-organized ministry, even of the family-based variety, has recently come under fire in evangelical circles. Youth ministry critics are nothing new. But the most recent hostility has come from "insiders"—youth and children's ministry educators and pastors—as well as disgruntled children of the youth ministry movement, mostly former youth pastors and speakers. These prophets of doom challenge the viability, and in some cases even the biblical validity, of age-organized ministry.

Here are a few of the criticisms made against youth ministry in the past few years:

- "Could it be that the paradigm itself is broken? Could it be that we have established systems designed to meet the wrong needs and attack the wrong problems. . . . The current approach isn't working."[5]
- "There is some bad news here, no question. . . . There is no easy way to say it, but it must be said. Parents and churches are not passing on a robust Christian faith and an accompanying commitment to the church."[6]

---

5. Baucham, *Family Driven Faith*, 176–82.
6. LifeWay Research, "Reasons 18 to 22 Year Olds Drop Out of Church": www.lifeway .com.

- "The curtain must be pulled back. If we are to keep young people involved in the church and if we are to renew our congregations, we first must acknowledge that many of our current forms of youth ministry are destructive."[7]
- "Discussions with colleagues and others led to the conclusion that current youth ministry has not been effective. The cottage industries related to youth ministry are, although financially lucrative, spiritually anemic."[8]
- "It's time for a thorough examination of our youth ministry philosophy and praxis."[9]
- "When we consider the investment that has been made in the lives of this generation of students, it is difficult to believe how many students are leaving evangelical churches and their faith. . . . With all of the time, money, and energy poured into teens, why are we not getting a better return on our investment?[10]

One common thread running through this vocal group of skeptics is that youth ministry is in serious trouble; perhaps it is even irreparably broken. In many cases age-segregated ministry is identified as one of the culprits. The obvious question that must be raised at this point is, "What is driving this group of people, many of whom love young people and have a long history with age-organized ministry, to sound such an alarm?"

## How Research into Age-Organized Ministry Has Been Inappropriately Used

There is one motivator that figures significantly into the majority of these claims: the infamous evangelical "dropout statistic." Ever heard of it? The dropout statistic has been quoted almost as gospel truth in ministry conferences, journal articles, and Web logs for about a decade now. A recent Internet search revealed nearly 250,000 references to the dropout statistic.

7. Yaconelli, "Youth Ministry," 450–53 (see chap. 2, n. 29).
8. Reid, *Raising the Bar*, 42 (see chap. 6, n. 112).
9. M. King, *Presence-Centered Youth Ministry* (Downers Grove, Ill.: InterVarsity, 2006), 11.
10. Wright and Graves, *reThink*, 21–22 (see chap. 4, n. 90).

This statistic is now functioning as a weapon to argue for the demolition of age-organized ministry, especially in ministries to adolescents. Almost without exception one impetus for lashing out against the age-organized philosophy that undergirds contemporary youth ministry begins with this supposed statistic. One critic states emphatically,

> According to researchers, between 70 and 88 percent of Christian teens are leaving the church by their second year in college. That's right, modern American Christianity has a failure rate somewhere around eight (almost nine) out of ten when it comes to raising children who continue in the faith. . . . The culture of secular humanism appears to have co-opted America's Christian teens.[11]

Mike King echoes this tone of alarm: "According to data from denominations and research organizations, a majority of youth are walking away from the institutional church when they reach late adolescence, and most don't come back."[12] Kara Powell and Krista Kubiak of Fuller Seminary summarize the dropout problem in this way: "Various denominations have estimated that between 65% and 94% of their high school students stop attending church after they graduate."[13]

Before demonstrating that age-organized family-based ministry represents the most viable form of family ministry, I want first to raise some questions about the cornerstone of the criticisms. I contend that the driving motivation behind sweeping critiques of current ministry practice has been based, for the most part, on a few tenuous statistics that are flawed or incomplete.

## Where Did These Numbers Come From?

There are five primary sources for the dropout statistics that the critics have quoted: the Barna Group,[14] youth ministry writ-

---

11. Baucham, *Family Driven Faith*, 10–12.
12. King, *Presence-Centered Youth Ministry*, 11.
13. K. Powell and K. Kubiak, "When the Pomp and Circumstance Fades," *Youthworker* (Sept.-Oct. 2005): 51.
14. See, e.g., G. Barna, *Today's Teens* (Glendale, Calif.: Barna Publishing Group, 1991). Barna quotes the results of a survey he conducted on the attendance patterns of

er and speaker Jay Strack,[15] the Southern Baptist Convention's Council on Family Life,[16] T. C. Pinckney's 2004 Christian Education Resolution,[17] and a 2007 study from LifeWay Research.[18] These sources reported dropout rates that ranged from 60 to 90 percent for evangelical teenagers in the years following their high school graduations. The statistics cited in these studies can be summarized with two simple words—*misleading* and *inconclusive*.

The dropout statistics are misleading because, in some cases, what is presented as hard evidence is actually based on anecdotes and personal experiences masquerading as evidence. Take, for example, the claim from the Council on Family Life that 88 percent of children from evangelical families drop out of church after high school. This number was drawn from the book *Family to Family*. And how did they obtain this statistic? This percentage was based on the experiences and recollections of a couple of youth ministry veterans, Jerry Pipes and Victor Lee.[19]

teenagers and young adults, where he found that church involvement declines notably during the young adult years.

15. In a personal interview with Jay Strack (September 2006), Strack stated that sometime in the early 1990s, he was simply articulating his own impressions of youth ministry when he mentioned that 90 percent of young people seemed to be leaving church after high school.

16. V. Lee and J. Pipes released a book entitled *Family to Family* (Alpharetta, Ga.: North American Mission Board, 1999) in which they stated that 88 percent of evangelical youth drop out of the church after high school graduation. This statistic was picked up and quoted numerous times during Southern Baptist Convention meetings in an attempt to call for withdrawal from government-sanctioned schools. For discussions of this issue see Baptist Press articles entitled "SBC Calls for Cultural Engagement; Education Resolution Declined" (June 2004): www.bpnews.net/BPnews.asp?ID=18501, and, "Family Life Council Says It's Time to Bring Family Back to Life" (June 2002): www.sbcannualmeeting.net/sbc02/newsroom/newspage.asp?ID=261.

17. T. C. Pinckney, "We Are Losing Our Children": www.schoolandstate.org/SBC/Pinckney WeAreLosingOurChildren.htm. In 2001, Pinckney reported to the Southern Baptist Convention's Executive Committee that "research indicates that 70% of teens who are involved in a church youth group will stop attending church within two years of their high school graduation." No actual research, however, was cited in his report.

18. LifeWay Research, "Reasons 18 to 22 Year Olds Drop Out." In 2007, LifeWay Research conducted a landmark study that found that 70 percent of young adults ages eighteen to twenty-two who had previously attended a Protestant church during high school reportedly dropped out of church for at least a year. This research was picked up and used in the 2007 SBC Report to the Executive Committee: "The overwhelming majority of children from evangelical families are leaving the church as they enter adulthood" (2007 SBC Annual Report, 168).

19. Lee and Pipes, *Family to Family*, 124.

In a personal interview with Jay Strack, he stated that his contribution to the dropout number came out of a gathering of denominational leaders, parachurch workers, and youth pastors. He asked these ministers to give their "gut feeling" on how many kids they were losing after high school graduation. He specifically stated that he never intended for this observation to be used as a published statistic.[20]

Even the few credible statistics about dropouts are ultimately inconclusive. Barna's research demonstrated only that church involvement tends to decline sharply among young adults; no correlation or connection was made between this statistic and age-organized ministry.

LifeWay Research did conduct some solid research into church dropout rates in 2007. LifeWay interviewed more than one thousand adults from ages eighteen to thirty and found that 70 percent reported dropping out of church for at least a year during their college years. While the validity of this study is well established, it is doubtful whether the data can be generalized to demonstrate any real problems with the prevailing age-organized youth ministry paradigm in evangelical churches.[21]

In the first place, LifeWay began with a mixed pool of sample participants, surveying all Protestant young adults without any reference to differences between liberal and conservative denominations. Mainline churches, which have been in decline for decades, were lumped together with growing conservative-evangelical denominations. Beyond this, LifeWay's definition of "church involvement" left much to be desired: Participants were said to have been involved in church if they attended church at least twice a month. Yet twice-a-month attendance is far from "active involvement" in a ministry. In my congregation those attending twice a month are considered evangelistic prospects or, at best, marginal attendees. In the statistics from LifeWay, churches were held responsible for dropouts that were never really theirs in the first place! As such, the 70 percent dropout rate reported by LifeWay is, at best, inconclusive when it comes to

---

20. Strack, personal interview.
21. This paragraph drawn from B. Shields, forthcoming work.

the question of whether present youth ministry paradigms are broken.[22]

And yet the statistics themselves aren't even the primary problem. Rather, it is how they are employed to bolster critics' claims about the ineffectiveness of current practices of ministry. Even if a large number of students *are* dropping out of church after high school, this does not necessarily mean that age-organized ministry is the culprit or that any certain form of family ministry represents the solution.

## A Reassessment of Dropout Rates

Because of the lack of usable data regarding postgraduation attrition rates, I recently engaged in a carefully designed study of church dropout rates. I surveyed hundreds of young adults from a dozen churches that had dynamic age-organized youth ministries. "Dynamic youth ministry" was defined as a youth ministry that had a minister who served in his or her position for at least five years, that held conservative-evangelical theological beliefs, and that engaged in intentional and systematic evangelism and discipleship. Furthermore, I developed four categories of youth ministry commitment to delineate the degree to which the young adults actually participated in their church's programs.

The research revealed that among teenagers who had been actively involved in dynamic youth ministries, 88 percent remained actively involved in local church contexts as young adults. More than half of these young adults now participate at high involvement levels by serving in leadership positions, actively engaging in spiritual disciplines, and being involved in mission trips. As commitment in the youth ministry increased, so did retention rates after high school. Approximately 93 percent of the high schoolers who were "engaged disciples" in their youth groups made the transition to active church involvement as young adults.[23] While these percentages represent only one

22. This paragraph drawn from B. Shields, forthcoming work.
23. B. Shields, "An Assessment of Dropout Rates of Former Youth Group Participants in Conservative Southern Baptist Megachurches" (Ph.D diss., The Southern Baptist Theological Seminary, 2008).

portion of a much larger picture, the retention rates in these churches do suggest that the supposed dropout statistics of between 70 and 88 percent may not necessarily demonstrate that present paradigms of ministry are irreparably broken. At the very least, it is clear that age-organized ministry is not the sole or primary cause of postgraduation church dropouts.

## Age-Organized Ministry as Missiological Opportunity

What, then, drives critics to exhibit such vocal opposition to age-organized ministry? Philosophically, many of these authors seem to possess a strong disdain for "age-graded" ministry, or what they call "systematic segregation." Voddie Baucham puts it this way:

> While I believe the vast majority of those who shepherd segregated portions of congregations are well meaning and would never presume to replace parents in their biblical role, I believe the modern American practice of systematic age segregation goes beyond the biblical mandate. I believe it is a product of the American educational system, and in some instances it actually works against families as opposed to helping them pursue multigenerational faithfulness.[24]

Such an attitude seems to suggest that segregating people into age-appropriate groups at church for three or so hours each week is tantamount to spiritual child abuse. By organizing ministries into age-appropriate groupings, churches cause parents to abdicate their God-given discipleship roles and to hand over their children to a secularized dog-and-pony show—or so these skeptics suggest.

I agree that, in an intact Christian family, parents are the persons primarily responsible to disciple their own children. I also agree that churches are responsible to call and equip Christian parents to become primary disciplers in their children's lives. The real question, however, is what place a biblically grounded auxiliary ministry—such as age-organized youth or children's

---

24. Baucham, *Family Driven Faith*, 178.

ministry—might have in the process of reaching and discipling young people. Critics of age-organized ministry claim that age-segmented auxiliary ministries should not provide the template for a church's organization; some critics even suggest that such auxiliary ministries are counterproductive and unbiblical.

Think with me for a moment. In a typical year even a churched youth only participates in thirty-five or forty age-organized programs.[25] At worst, age-organized church activities merely accentuate other more formative factors such as family and school environments. At their best, however, age-organized programs function as vital missiological tools to touch the hearts of lost students who would not otherwise have a chance to respond in faith to the gospel. This passion for the use of age-appropriate family-based programs to reach the greatest number of students is more than mere pragmatic reflex; it is rooted in the missional character and nature of God Himself.

## Models of Age-Organized Ministry that Prevent Family-Based Ministry

I am not defending the value or the validity of *all* age-organized ministries. Age-organized ministry does have its shortcomings. It would be similar to the challenge of keeping your body in tip-top physical shape when even commendable regimens can be taken to unhealthy extremes and cause more harm than good. Just as there are diets and exercise regimens that can cause harm to one's physical body, there are forms of age-organized ministries that are harmful and unhealthy for the body of Christ.

Family-based ministry requires refocusing the church's ministry programs. Part of this refocusing process requires that churches move away from three unhealthy age-organized ministry models: activity-driven ministry, uni-generational ministry, and culturally immersed ministry.

---

25. A. Stanley and S. Hall, *Max Q: Developing Students of Influence* (West Monroe, La.: Howard Books, 2004), 27–28.

## Family-Based Focus Requires Movement
## Away from Activity-Driven Ministry

Family-based churches see no reason to abandon age-organized retreats, camps, short-term mission trips, small-group discipleship environments, and even "nonspiritual" events that facilitate preevangelism by building relationships. At the same time, if any ministry becomes enamored with drawing crowds or with entertaining students at the expense of disciple-making, the results will be disastrous.

All cotton candy and no meat. For the last two decades, this seems to have been the prevailing perception of youth ministries, especially in megachurches. Take, for example, this recent article from *Time* magazine:

> Youth ministers have been on a long and frustrating quest of their own over the past two decades or so. Believing that a message wrapped in pop-culture packaging was the way to attract teens to their flocks, pastors watered down the religious content and boosted the entertainment. . . . Sugar-coated Christianity, popular in the 1980s and early '90s, has caused growing numbers of kids to turn away not just from attending youth-fellowship activities but also from practicing their faith at all.[26]

Activity-driven youth ministries are easy to spot. They are programmatically heavy, theologically confused, philosophically shallow, and have a high rate of staff turnover.

In terms of family ministry, activity-driven programs are problematic because they usually see themselves in competition with, and not supplemental to, parents in the task of discipling youth and children. Instead of developing dynamic partnerships for discipleship, the relationship between church and family resembles a discipleship factory: Parents expect to plug their kids into the church's activities and to receive, a few years later, an eighteen-year-old Christian young adult. When this doesn't happen, the result is frustration, blame-shifting, and conflict. Such

---

26. S. Steptoe, "In Touch with Jesus," *Time Magazine* (2006): www.time.com/time/magazine/printout/0,8816,1552027,00.html.

FAMILY-BASED MINISTRY — **109**

a misguided focus is antithetical to the family-based ministry model. In the final analysis, family-based ministry is *not* activity-driven ministry.

## Family-Based Focus Requires Movement Away from Uni-Generational Ministry

Several years ago, I had the privilege of speaking to a group of teenagers in one of the fastest-growing churches in the South. As I walked into the student facility, a sharp young woman in her twenties greeted me and directed me to the room where a pre-service meeting with youth leaders would take place.

When I entered the room, I was surprised to discover I was one of the oldest people in the room—and I was only twenty-six at the time! The majority of the volunteers were in their early twenties and extremely hip, with black thin-rimmed glasses, well-gelled hair, and sentences that always contained "like" and somehow always ended in "bro."

Too many churches act as if it is impossible to reach teenagers with anyone not under the age of thirty and who does not maintain killer social-networking pages. Such churches hire underqualified youth ministers who then recruit college students and recent high school graduates to boost their coolness factor. Before long, a group of youth leaders is developed who look for Bon Jovi songs in the "oldies" section.

Leadership in a family-based church cannot be uni-generational because family-based churches work consistently and intentionally to build intergenerational relationships. In a family-based church, seasoned adult mentors contact, care for, and connect with students week after week.

To be sure, there is nothing inherently wrong with enlisting a twenty-something as a mentor in youth or children's ministry. But if the bulk of workers in a ministry are within a decade of their teenaged years, something is seriously wrong. The Bible clearly couches discipleship in multigenerational terms (Titus 2:1–8), suggesting that a network of grandparents, empty nesters, young couples, college students, single moms, widows, and widowers provides the best context for effective discipleship outside an intact family unit. Young people desperately need to develop wisdom and biblical maturity. In family-based churches, relationships with a variety of age groupings build these qualities into the lives of children and teenagers.

### Family-Based Focus Requires Movement Away from Culturally Immersed Ministry

During my senior year of college, I served as a youth ministry intern in a large congregation in Kentucky. The church had just taken responsibility for a satellite campus in a fast-growing area of Louisville, and I was shipped off to start a student ministry from scratch. With no students, no facility, and virtually no budget, I needed to get creative. So I began visiting other churches to see what I could glean from well-established ministries.

A church down the street had a reputation for being a hip place; everywhere I went, I heard teenagers talking about this particular nondenominational ministry. On the Sunday evening I visited, I noticed the typical amenities of a trendy youth ministry: a large gathering space outfitted with cozy furniture, various provisions for entertainment, and cutting-edge technology. During the opening moments of the service, the lights dimmed, and the band rocked out with a song from the Dave Matthews Band entitled "Don't Drink the Water." Throughout the song students moshed and danced. When the song concluded, there was no explanation of the racist lyrics, and no meaningful connections were made to any biblical truth. I immediately concluded that this was not the way to grow a youth ministry. What was happening here was no different than the over-twenty-one bar where my unsaved friends got wasted on the weekends, except that there was no alcohol being served here. This ministry had utterly immersed itself in the culture—the same music, the same message, and the same confusion about what Jesus came to do.

When attempting to reach another culture, there is a fine line between *relevance* and *accommodation*. In an attempt to become missionaries who present a relevant message, many age-organized ministries fail to evaluate their methods. In the process they lose their biblical distinctiveness. Missiologists call this "going native." As cultural commentator Walt Mueller points out:

> When we believe that we must adapt our faith by following the culture's lead, it is the world that is setting the agenda for the church. When we fall prey to this subtle seduction, what is viewed as "normal" or statistically "average" becomes what's right and the distinctives of the faith disappear.[27]

Any ministry immersed in the world's culture is dangerous. Watered-down biblical teaching inevitably contributes to weak-kneed Christian students with few convictions. Students in culturally immersed churches fail to find support, encouragement, and accountability in their youth ministries. Instead, they discover new temptations, sinful habits, and unhealthy friendships with peers who model values that are antithetical to a biblical worldview.

Genuine family-based ministry is not activity driven, unigenerational, or culturally immersed. Each of these three extremes diminishes meaningful family connections and undercuts parental efforts at discipleship. Age-organized ministry is not, however, the cause of these negative results! These negative results are caused by poorly strategized implementation of age-organized ministry—implementation that stands in direct opposition to authentic family-based ministry.

The high school ministry in my church offers a strategic variety of fun and serious events for high schoolers; we design these events to draw students to deeper levels of kingdom living. Over the years we have seen hundreds of students converted, challenged, inspired, and called to ministry through these events. Last year, in a series of focus groups with key parents, I asked this question: "What has had the most significant spiritual impact on your high school student?" Immediately, the parents began to name key events where their students sensed God speaking to them in a compelling way. These programs and events, while not an end in themselves, provided students with a "hook" that

---

27. W. Mueller, *Engaging the Soul of Youth Culture* (Downers Grove, Ill.: InterVarsity Press, 2006) 139–40.

helped them connect a specific need in their lives with the calling of Jesus Christ.

Simply because a congregation's programs include age-organized events does not mean that the church neglects intergenerational relationships or leadership. In my church hundreds of teenage boys are being raised without fathers, or their fathers are spiritually absent. I remember one troubled youth who came to us with a messed-up home life. His single mother was doing the best she could, with little social capital and with intrinsic skepticism when it came to male authority figures. Through our Sunday morning small groups, the boy connected with a deacon who became a mentor and father figure for this desperate young man. The result was a twelve-year journey wherein this deacon led the boy to trust Jesus, nurtured his physical and spiritual development, and taught him to be a man. As an adult, this young man has now sensed a calling to full-time ministry. He serves on our music ministry staff and plans to attend seminary after finishing his undergraduate degree. Such stories are not isolated anecdotes; they are common experiences in our family-based church.

## What Makes Family-Based Ministry Different from Other Family Ministry Models

The family-based model differs from some other family ministry models on at least three significant issues: how the regulative principle of church order is applied, how the priority of evangelism ought to shape ministry practices, and what Christian compassion requires.

### How the Regulative Principle Is Applied

The regulative principle contends that everything done in the church must be prescribed by Scripture. Reformed theologians have traditionally held this view; they have usually applied the regulative principle to the elements, order, and functions of worship.[28]

---

28. See J. Frame, "A Fresh Look at the Regulative Principle": thirdmill.org and M. Bushell, *The Songs of Zion* (Pittsburgh, Penn.: Crown and Covenant, 1980).

Opponents of youth and children's ministry have appealed to the regulative principle and adamantly declared that age-segregated models have "no clear biblical mandate"[29] and are largely "unbiblical."[30] Voddie Baucham cut to the heart of this concern in a blog posting:

> What I have never had is a conversation with a person presenting the argument for segregated youth [and] children's ministry from an open Bible. I have never had a professor, a student, a youth pastor, or anyone else show me book, chapter, and verse in defense of the contemporary model.[31]

This "logic" is faulty and dangerous. By this reasoning a biblical church is one that can trace every form, expression, and practice to a specific biblical text. The argument is ironic, given the fact that the leaders who raise these criticisms employ many extrabiblical tools in their ministries, ranging from Web sites and blogs to confessions of faith and vision statements.

These critics hold an extremely selective perspective on the regulative principle. In so doing, they have wrongly labeled age-organized ministries as unbiblical. Every church uses cultural forms to articulate timeless truths in its own cultural context. Since the Bible contains no itemized handbook for church organization and practice, each church is responsible to extrapolate broader theological principles that form the parameters for their ministry efforts.

Does age-organized ministry have a biblical mandate? No. I can't find a verse in the Bible that prescribes the present forms of youth or children's ministry. This does not imply, however, that there is no theological basis for a church choosing to structure ministries in an age-graded and family-based manner. In fact, I believe that shifts in Western culture demand the establishment of youth ministry and other age-organized practices of ministry.

---

29. Baucham, *Family Driven Faith*, 179.
30. Vision Forum Ministries, "A Biblical Confession for Uniting Church and Family": www.visionforumministries.org.
31. V. Baucham, "Answering Objections on the YM Issue" (October 2006): www.voddiebaucham.org/blog.

Age-organized, family-based ministry exists as a tool to address cultural ills in relevant and practical ways.

## How the Priority of Evangelism Ought to Shape Ministry Practices

Modern youth ministry traces its roots to the mid-nineteenth century. It began as a response to what many people called the "youth problem"—large populations of uneducated, poor, and spiritually disinterested young people between the ages of sixteen and forty. There were no formal and intentional programs for reaching young people with the gospel. As Mark Senter notes, "Changes in culture gave birth to a program which was quickly grounded in theory."[32]

Forerunners of youth ministry such as Theodore Cuyler and Francis Clark attempted to address the "youth problem" in a number of innovative ways. These innovations led to organizations like the Young People's Society of Christian Endeavor and the Young People's Association. All of these organizations began as attempts to evangelize young people.[33]

Near the end of the nineteenth century, the Industrial Revolution drew scores of young people to American cities in search of jobs. Around this time, psychologist G. Stanley Hall began to view young people as a culturally distinctive group. Within a few decades, compulsory public education became a growing phenomenon in American culture.[34] As these factors combined, the culture came to include a subculture of teenagers who spent large amounts of time interacting with their peers apart from their nuclear family units.

Faced with this sociological shift, those engaging in ministry among young people in the youth culture began to view themselves as missionaries to a "foreign" culture. While churches responded slowly to the changing cultural tide, parachurch organizations stepped in and developed aggressive programs for

---

32. M. Senter III, "Horace Bushnell, Theodore Cuyler, and Francis Clark: A Study of How Youth Ministry Began," *The Journal of Youth Ministry* 2 (2004): 31.

33. Ibid., 48.

34. For an insightful introduction to this phenomenon see T. Hine, *The Rise and Fall of the American Teenager* (Toronto, Canada: HarperCollins, 1999).

outreach that specifically addressed the needs and challenges
facing American teenagers.[35]

Beginning in the 1960s, the sexual revolution sparked another cultural shift as people refashioned previous patterns of sexual
behavior and family expectations. Freed by the birth-control pill
from much of the perceived baggage that previous generations
connected with sexual intercourse, people began to tolerate and
even to promote adjustments in traditional behavioral norms.
In the decades following the sexual revolution, cohabitation
rates spiraled from 30 percent to over 67 percent,[36] no-fault divorce became increasingly prevalent,[37] birth rates plummeted by
43 percent,[38] and the number of children growing up without
an intact nuclear family skyrocketed to epidemic proportions.
Researcher Thom Rainer describes the struggle well:

> Never has a generation of Americans been raised in such
> difficult family environments. . . . But the church cannot
> simply give lip service to welcoming a generation with many
> dysfunctional persons. It must provide ministries that touch
> the heart and the needs of hurting people. . . . This will re-
> quire that the church allocate significant resources to stu-
> dent and children's ministries.[39]

In response to such seismic social shifts, churches reevalu-
ated their responsibilities. The new face of the American family
drove churches in the 1960s and 1970s to refocus organizational
infrastructures to promote children's ministries, junior high
ministries, and high school ministries in an effort to reach these
age demographics more effectively. Youth ministries identified
points of common ground with culture in an attempt to be more
aggressively evangelistic.

35. Senter III, *Coming Revolution*, 108–20 (see chap. 3, n. 58).

36. J. Arnett, *Emerging Adulthood* (New York: Oxford University, 2004), 5.

37. T. Rainer, *The Bridger Generation* (Nashville, Tenn.: B&H, 1997), 53. Rainer also
points out that the United States has the highest divorce rate of any nation in the developed world.

38. A. Mohler, "Deliberate Childlessness: Moral Rebellion with a New Face": www
.albertmohler.com/commentary_read.php?cdate=2003-10-13.

39. Rainer, *Bridger Generation*, 52–65.

Family-based churches are acutely aware of the prevailing youth culture and of the breakdown of the nuclear family. Such churches see these trends as strategic opportunities for pursuing the Great Commission in the context of age-organized youth and children's ministries. These churches take seriously the words of the apostle Paul: "I have become all things to all people, so that I may by every possible means save some. Now I do all this because of the gospel, so I may become a partner in its benefits" (1 Cor 9:22–23).

## What Christian Compassion Requires

The Bible presents a clear and consistent message that God's people are responsible to demonstrate compassion for orphans and widows (Exod 22:22; Jer 49:11; Jas 1:27) and others in diverse, difficult, and damaged families. Think about the people God used throughout the Bible from a diversity of family backgrounds, including Moses, who was adopted by Pharaoh's daughter, Ruth, who came from a different culture, Rahab the former prostitute, and Hosea, who loved an unfaithful wife.

In our culture this calling to show compassion compels us to minister to a myriad of divergent and nontraditional family structures: orphaned children, single moms and dads, divorced and blended families, teenagers with spiritually absent parents, households with two working parents, and so on. Family-based churches believe that God has commissioned the local church to reach all people, in all family contexts, in every nation, with the gospel of Jesus (Matt 28:18–20; Acts 1:8).

Family-based churches agree with other family ministry models on a number of issues, such as biblical manhood and womanhood, the need for parents to disciple their children, and the responsibility of fathers to lead in their homes. Yet family-based churches take it a step further in that they recognize the evangelistic responsibility of the church extends beyond the doors of Christian homes.

In our society the intact nuclear family is quickly becoming a cultural minority. Presently, 28 percent of elementary and high school students live in single-parent circumstances. The Great

Commission requires Christians to engage people from many family settings for the purposes of evangelism and discipleship, and Scripture seems to grant freedom for churches to organize themselves in a variety of ways to accomplish this mission. While churches should be led by biblically qualified pastors, there is nothing in the Bible prohibiting the promotion of age-graded ministries or the delegation of responsibilities for different age groups to a multiplicity of ministers.[40]

## Family-Based Ministry: Positioned for Maximum Kingdom Impact

Family-based churches are in the best position to model both theologically and practically God's radical love for all kinds of people. Here are a couple of examples to demonstrate why family-based ministry is the most effective means for organizing a church to share the gospel with the greatest number of people.

### Jason and Sarah

Jason and Sarah were in their thirties, and their lives were a mess spiritually, morally, and financially. As a couple, they had a complicated religious background that included stints in other faiths. Previously, they were heavily involved in drugs. Now they were a blended family with multiple stepchildren from previous marriages. Both worked ordinary lower middle-class jobs to make ends meet, and they sent their kids to local public schools. Recently, Jason and Sarah received the message of Jesus Christ and began the process of finding a church where they could connect.

If they had shown up on Sunday in a church emphasizing family integration, what do you think might happen? They would look around and notice that intact, Christian family units predominate in this fellowship. They probably would not find anyone to help them to deal with their children because they would be expected to keep their children with them throughout all or

---

40. Some language in the two previous paragraphs alludes to D. Adams and J. Scroggins, "The Strategic Family Ministry Model": www.thecym.com.

part of the worship service. The children would bicker loudly, utterly unable to track with the preacher's message. Around the lunch table Jason and Sarah would fumble their way through awkward conversations about where they attended college (neither of them finished), where they live (a blue-collar neighborhood on the other side of town), and where their children attend school. Jason and Sarah would quickly discover that most of these people are well-educated, upper-middle-class homeschoolers. The conversation might or might not end with other families expressing a desire to help this young couple. How do you think Jason and Sarah's experience in this congregation would have felt? More than likely they would have gone home discouraged. Everyone else seemed to have it together, and there were no families facing the same struggles as theirs.

Now consider what did happen when they attended a nearby family-based congregation. In adult Sunday school, they were able to focus on the lesson while their children attended a different small group. There Jason and Sarah discovered that a number of couples came from blended marriages with homes like theirs. During worship Jason and Sarah's younger children participated in an enjoyable, high-energy worship celebration that leaders had carefully designed to make sense to children. The volunteer staff in the children's and youth ministries included seasoned Christian adults who took on their children and helped them to get started in the discipleship process.

For the first time Jason and Sarah's children actually enjoyed going to church—the environment was fun, they made Christian friends, and their teachers cared about them. Who knows? With time maybe Jason and Sarah will gain sufficient spiritual momentum and maturity to start a blended couples Sunday school class with the purpose of reaching couples who face unique family challenges.

### Richard and Terri

Middle-aged Richard and Terri had two children and attended an age-organized church. Richard's work ethic has enabled his family to enjoy the perks of the upper middle class. He is extremely interested in theology, and he reads the works of past and present religious authors. Richard and Terri have networked with a group of like-minded families who are convinced that homeschooling represents the best educational option for their children.

Richard and Terri have become increasingly frustrated with their church's youth ministry. When they drop their kids off at the midweek worship service, they are appalled at the crude language other teenagers casually drop in conversations. Terri, who works hard to teach her daughter the value of modesty, cannot believe that mothers would let their daughters leave home in such short skirts and low-cut tops. In fact, it is the kind of messed-up, nontraditional families represented by these youth that Richard and Terri are trying to steer their family away from. "This youth ministry is out of control," Richard concludes on the way home that night. He and Terri decide it is time to check out some other church options.

When they visit one particular congregation, Richard and Terri are surrounded by intact families with well-disciplined and well-behaved children. Immediately they feel at home. This congregation, with its consistent focus on discipleship at home and on doctrine-rich messages, represented everything Richard thought church should be. Here his family could learn together without dealing with messed-up families or watered-down preaching.

## The Need for Family-Based Churches

For households like Richard and Terri's, family-integrated and family-equipping ministry models seem extremely attractive. Unfortunately, statistics and common sense combine to suggest that families like Richard and Terri's are a cultural minority both in mainstream culture and in the narrower evangelical subculture. Jason and Sarah—the first parents I described—are far closer to the typical family in America. They most likely would not feel welcomed in a church that's filled with intact, upper-middle class, homeschooling families. Such congregations serve a tiny subgroup of evangelicals, but they fail to exemplify the diversity that should be expected in an evangelistically aggressive body of believers.

Family-based churches, however, are theologically and practically positioned for maximum gospel impact in today's culture. By strategically organizing around age-focused ministries, family-based churches can reach out directly to youth and children to make Jesus known in the heart of the culture. In this model orphans, single parents, blended families, struggling addicts, and outcasts have the best chance of hearing the message of Jesus.

This does not mean that the church ignores the importance of discipleship in the home. Family-based churches teach and model biblical manhood and womanhood, marital fidelity, proper family roles, and family discipleship. In a family-based church, however, it isn't either-or but both-and. "Let the little children come to Me," Jesus said to his disciples. "Don't stop them, for the kingdom of God belongs to such as these" (Mark 10:14). Perhaps it was children from families like Jason and Sarah's that Jesus had in mind when he spoke these words.

CHAPTER 8

# *Responses to Brandon Shields*
## Family-Based Ministry

## *Response by Paul Renfro*

It's encouraging to see how the family-based model tries to reorient present models of programming to point church members toward intergenerational interaction. So many American families are merely a shell of what God created them to be. In such families each family member has personal agendas and schedules; homes are merely pit stops for the washing of clothes, the provision of food, and a few hours of sleep. Anything done to reconnect families in such a culture is helpful. I am also encouraged by Shields's clear recognition that parents are the persons primarily responsible for the discipleship of their children. At the same time, I see three specific problems in this presentation. First, there is a greater concern for relevance in the culture than for faithfulness to Scripture. Second, there is a failure to recognize the inadequacy of evangelism focusing primarily on children and youth. And third, there is little if any clear and consistent training of parents to serve as primary disciple-makers in their children's lives.

## Sola Scriptura or Sola Cultura?

In his defense of family-based ministry, Brandon Shields admits that no specific Scripture "prescribes the present forms of youth or children's ministry." Yet he also contends that shifts in Western culture demand the establishment of youth ministry and other age-segregated ministry paradigms. According to his family-based perspective, age-segregated ministry "exists as a tool to address cultural ills in relevant and practical ways." Yet, if shifts in Western culture actually demand that a church structure itself in specific ways not mandated in Scripture simply to address cultural ills, that congregation's locus of authority has shifted from *sola Scriptura* ("Scripture only") to *cultura et Scriptura* ("culture and Scripture") or even *sola cultura* ("culture only").

In *The Courage to Be Protestant,* theologian David Wells addresses the emergence of *sola cultura* as the authority in many churches:

> In the last two or three decades evangelicals have discovered culture. That actually sounds more flattering than I intend. I would welcome a serious discussion about culture. We should be exploring what it is and how it works, rather than just looking at polls to see what is hot.
>
> A serious engagement with culture, though, is not what most evangelicals are about. . . . They have no interest at all in what lies beneath the trends. . . . Pragmatists to the last drop of blood, these evangelicals are now in the cultural waters, not to understand what is there, but to get some movement. . . . This quest for success, which passes under the language of "relevance," is what is partitioning the evangelical world. . . . The issue that has emerged . . . is whether evangelicals will build their churches *sola Scriptura* or *sola cultura.* . . . What is the binding authority on the church? What determines how it thinks, what it wants, and how it is going to go about its business? Will it be Scripture alone, Scripture understood as God's binding address, or will it be culture? Will it be what is current, edgy, and with-it? Or will it be God's Word, which is always contemporary because its

truth endures for all eternity? Of course I know that the issue does not present itself in this way. Evangelicals who live *sola cultura* all claim to be living *sola Scriptura*.[1]

David Wells is spot on—and *sola cultura* is precisely the problem with family-based ministry.

According to Shields, "the Bible contains no itemized handbook for church organization and practice"; therefore, "each church is responsible to extrapolate broader theological principles that form the parameters for their ministry efforts." Evidently, these extrapolations can be based on the demands of culture. Yet Scripture *does* clearly address how the church does her business, as Shields even admits! He rightly identifies three patterns of age-segregated ministry—activity driven, uni-generational, and culturally immersed—as "unhealthy for the body of Christ." Yet, if Scripture does *not* provide us with a regulative handbook for church organization and practice, why are these approaches considered unhealthy? If indeed "the Bible contains no itemized handbook for church organization and practice" and if "each church is responsible to extrapolate broader theological principles," what is the problem with these approaches? Don't these churches have the freedom to do whatever seems best to reach unbelievers? In defense of developing ministry models that adapt to demands of culture, Shields cites 1 Corinthians 9:22–23. Yet this text refers to individuals giving up individual Christian liberties to gain an audience with the lost, not to adapting church structures to the culture for the sake of evangelism.

According to this family-based minister, it is faulty and dangerous to seek a biblical example for every aspect of a church's order; he takes family-integrated churches to task for holding to the regulative principle while employing "many extrabiblical tools in their ministries, ranging from Web sites and blogs to confessions of faith and vision statements." Yet the author takes the statement from Voddie Baucham about "chapter and verse" completely out of context. Elsewhere, even in the post that Shields cites, Baucham has clarified his intent. In *Family Driven Faith,* he puts it this way:

1. Wells, *Courage*, 3–4 (see chap. 5, n. 105).

I fully recognize that many of the things we do in church today are not found in the Bible. We would be hard-pressed to find a church building (as we know it), a pulpit, or a microphone in the book of Acts. So I am not arguing that the fact that something is not specifically mentioned in Scripture means it is absolutely forbidden in today's church.[2]

What is truly faulty and dangerous is abandoning the solid rock of *sola Scriptura* and attempting to navigate the constantly changing cultural waters without being solidly anchored to God's Word. Family-based ministry, though not as extreme in its culture-rootedness as many age-segregated models, still derives heavily from culture. As such, it remains an insufficient tool for the development of mature disciples of Jesus Christ. Thankfully, the Lord did not abandon methods of discipleship to the best of human intentions or to the latest fads of contemporary culture. Instead, he formed a fundamental social context for the evangelism of unbelievers and the discipleship of believers, and that fundamental context is the family.

### The Problem with Age-Segregated Evangelism

Brandon Shields claims that "family-based churches recognize that the evangelistic responsibility of the church extends beyond the doors of Christian homes." At this point I must ask, "Does Brandon really believe that family-based ministry is the only, or even the *primary*, model of family ministry that actively evangelizes outside the context of Christian families?" Throughout his chapter, he constructs a family-integrated straw man (or, perhaps more precisely, a "straw church"). This nonexistent "straw church" possesses little desire to proclaim the life-transforming gospel of Jesus Christ. Rather, it serves as a haven for intact families who do not want the broken families of our culture touching them. Nothing could be further from the truth when it comes to real-life family-integrated churches! Wherever you find a church that trains and expects parents to disciple their children, you will also find maturing believers who are passionate about taking the gospel to the darkest corners of the world.

---

2. Baucham, *Family Driven Faith*, 179.

That is the true character of a Spirit-led, Scripture-regulated, Christ-centered, family-integrated church.

Shields also implies that including broken families in the church ("blended marriages with homes like theirs") helps the church to evangelize broken families. Now I wholeheartedly agree that broken families should be evangelized and included in the congregation! Yet are intact families really less effective in reaching broken families? Could it be that well-ordered, intact families might offer hope and help to families broken and besieged by crumbling cultural norms? Could it be that what struggling families need is mentoring and loving guidance from husbands and wives who are discipling their children and whose families are intact? If one follows Brandon's implication that intact families are less effective in reaching broken families to its conclusion, the inevitable inference would be that the more we conform our lives to the commands of Scripture, the less able we will be to reach unbelievers. Viewed in this way, a lifetime of holiness would be a hindrance to the spread of the gospel instead of a help! I reject the notion that intact families are somehow disadvantaged when it comes to sharing the message of Christ with shattered or struggling families.

What about the claim that family-based ministry is preferable because of its supposed capacity to evangelize youth culture? The problem with this claim is that the most effective evangelistic strategies focus not on youth culture but on *parents*—and, specifically, on *fathers*. According to one reputable study, if a child or youth becomes a believer in Jesus Christ, there is only a 3.5 percent chance that the rest of the family will follow. If the mother becomes a Christian, the probability increases to 17 percent. If the father trusts Jesus, however, the entire family comes to faith in 93 percent of cases![3] And this doesn't appear to be a recent phenomenon: In the book of Acts, when Cornelius the centurion and the Philippian jailer became believers, their entire families followed suit (Acts 10; 16). Evangelism of youth and children in isolation from their families is not nearly as effective as evangelism that calls fathers and mothers to faith and then prepares

---

3. P. House, "Want Your Church to Grow? Then Bring in Men": www.bpnews.net.

them to evangelize and to disciple their families. As men's ministry specialist Sid Woodruff has pointed out, "There is something in the hard-wiring of creation that naturally causes wives and children to look to husbands and fathers to lead out."[4]

## What about Training the Parents?

I applaud the intention of the family-based model to connect children and parents through shared activities and service. Yet there seems to be little consistent parent training that equips fathers and mothers to become the primary disciplers in their children's lives. Christian Smith has pointed out:

> Religion seems to become rather compartmentalized and backgrounded in the lives and experiences of most U.S. teenagers. . . . This is not surprising. It simply reflects the fact that there is very little built-in religious content or connection in the structure of most U.S. adolescent's daily schedule and routines. Most U.S. teens' lives are dominated by school and homework.[5]

Age-segregated discipleship, punctuated by occasional intergenerational events, perpetuates this compartmentalization. What are needed are not merely events putting parents and youth together but intentional training so fathers and mothers can build discipleship into their children's daily lives.

God has entrusted the primary discipleship of children to parents—whether in intact, blended, or single-parent households. Why not simply trust God's wisdom and equip parents to do the job He has called them to do? When a church pursues this path, pastors and people alike come to understand the blessing that the Puritan pastor Richard Baxter proclaimed: "Get masters of families to do their duty, and they will not only spare you a great deal of labor, but will much further the success of your labors. . . . You are not likely to see any general reformation, till you procure family reformation."[6]

---

4. www.mobaptist.org/baptistmen.
5. Smith and Denton, *Soul Searching*, 130–31 (see chap. 5, n. 101).
6. R. Baxter, *The Reformed Pastor*, 93: books.google.com.

## Response by Jay Strother

Let me be up front from the start: The family-equipping model is in reality the younger brother of the family-based model. This little brother is growing up quickly with a somewhat different approach to life, but he stems from the same original DNA. I first read *Family-Based Youth Ministry* by Mark DeVries when I was just a couple of years into ministry. That book shaped my thinking in crucial ways, just as it did for many other youth ministers in my generation. In those early days I was well intentioned, but I had in my immaturity developed a subtle bias against parents. I saw the *problems* with the parents, but I had failed thus far to see them as part of the *solution*.

When I read these words by Mark DeVries, I began to see parents in a new light: "There is no such thing as a successful youth ministry that isolates teenagers from the community of faith."[7] Building on that point, Mark DeVries outlined a vision challenging churches to elevate a partnership with parents to the position of first priority and to make developing the "extended family" of the church the next priority. Early in my vocation as a student minister, I got these two in reverse order, and this accounted for much of my frustration. I and my band of youth workers could never quite seem to do enough to meet the growing needs around us, and I quickly discovered that I was not alone in that sense of frustration. Other youth pastors sensed the same tension in their ministries.

It took a decade or so to get to the point where we are now, but the spark that Mark DeVries, Richard Ross, Reggie Joiner, and others ignited has now captured the attention of evangelical churches throughout North America. Over the past five years or so, it seems as if the crucial question has shifted from "So what are you doing to attract kids to church?" to "So what are you doing to reach parents and then reconnect them to their kids?" We in family-equipping ministry are part of a courageous course correction that has been long overdue. We owe much to that initial generation of family-based leaders who were willing to challenge the popular paradigms of "religious edutainment" that

---

7. DeVries, *Family-Based Youth Ministry*, 103 (see chap. 1, n. 1).

dominated the ministry landscape for too long. Children and student ministries with solid attractions produced great attendance but too few true disciples of Christ.

As family-based ministry has matured, it has continued to develop in ways that benefit all of us. First, the stated core values of flexibility and balance are vital to the mission of any New Testament church seeking to reach families. Flexibility is another way of recognizing that the church today must consider its culture missionally. In God's providence the genius of the church is that its foundation rests on biblical principles that may be transferred to any culture and any setting. In the case of family ministry, the guiding biblical truth is that the faith of children is designed to be nurtured in homes of faith surrounded by a community of faith. Instead of cursing the darkness surrounding so many families, family-based churches attempt to be a light that leads families to a better way.

A second strength of the family-based model, especially as it is presented here, is that it pursues its calling without being distracted by alarmist rhetoric. The misuse of statistics documented in Brandon's chapter is indicative of a larger problem in the North American church, which is the measurements used to define ministry "success." In the first place, from a New Testament perspective, it is an improper practice to focus on "church attendance" as a primary tool for evaluating spiritual impact on a generation. Jesus never counted the size of the crowds attending His teaching sessions to assess His success. (In accounts of the miraculous feedings such as Matt 14:21, the evangelists provided estimates of four thousand and five thousand so readers could understand the enormity of the crowd and the context for the story, but it is clear from John 6:66 that the size of the crowds was not intended to measure Jesus' success.)

For planning purposes, it is a good leadership practice to track the persons attending our churches because each number represents, after all, a person who matters to God. Yet we have developed an unhealthy obsession with such statistics in North American churches. In a society obsessed with the latest trends, numbers can be used to coerce and to manipulate churches in unwholesome ways. There is no doubt that we are not where we need to be regarding this generation's spiritual formation, and perhaps statistics can help us understand some of these realities. It is, however, unhealthy to make radical assertions or to advocate wholesale changes without carefully examining what these numbers truly mean.

This leads me to a third benefit of family-based ministry: it can be adapted and done well in almost any church setting. The family-based church sees that the model alone is not what makes the difference. What makes the difference is how effectively the church applies biblical principles in the context of whatever model God leads them to pursue. The family-based church has sufficient flexibility to explore in its own context and unique church culture the best way to engage families and to reconnect parents with their children and students.

### Possible Problems in the Family-based Church

There is no doubt that the family-based movement began pushing the conversations about the church-home relationship to the forefront, and for this I am grateful. Yet, as I examine the model in today's context, I must ask, *Does family-based ministry go far enough, in actual practice, in addressing the disconnect between the church and family?*

Let me be blunt about our present predicament. Most parents, even Christian parents, are perfectly content to sit back and allow the church to assume the role of primary spiritual caregiver in their children's lives. In the typical church it will require significant changes not only in the message communicated to parents but also in the church's internal paradigms to send a loud and clear message that parents have the primary responsibility for their children's discipleship. "Action to bring about a change comes only after a *series* of changes in attitude."[8] This series of steps requires raising people's awareness of the problem, communicating the importance of the change, and elevating the families' level of concern to bring about a state of dissatisfaction with the present reality. Unless the vision is

---

8. From *Model-netics by Main Event Management Corporation*: www.modelnetics .com.

clearly and consistently communicated all the way up to this point of concern, many parents will never become aware that the church or the staff believes in parental responsibility for children's discipleship at all.

Family-based ministry creates venues and events that, in the words of Mark DeVries, provide "kids and adults excuses to interact together."[9] That's what Brandon Shields seems to be describing in the "Becoming a Man" series that lasts a few weeks in his congregation, as well as in the "Joy Prom." While such events and short-term programs represent great first steps, they are not sufficiently consistent or intentional to sustain the sort of family ministry so desperately needed.

Another related question that must be asked of the family-based church: *Where do you draw the line when it comes to programs and events?* This model often simply adds more activities that make families' already-busy lives even busier. When you add a "family-based" opportunity such as a Sunday night class for fathers and sons, what do you take away to create the needed time, space, and leadership for this program? Family-based churches are good at adding programs and events to their plates, but few are adept at moving things off those plates. It is typically only a matter of time until the plate becomes so full that something gets dropped, and what gets dropped is often the primacy of ministry to parents. Ministry to parents is not nearly as "flashy" as big events with big budgets and big crowds. As such, it becomes too easy to fail to provide parents with what they need in order to reorient their families toward home discipleship. Family-based ministry has helped to head the church in the right direction, but this model of ministry fails to go far enough in equipping parents to serve as primary disciple-makers in their children's lives.

## Potential Problems in the Family-Based Church

If family-based ministry merely represents how a church does *youth ministry,* this approach will simply not be sufficient. Unless the entire church staff buys into the family-based vision,

9. M. DeVries, et al., Youth Ministry Architects Web site: www.ymarchitects.com/resources.html.

there are likely to be issues with consistency and accountability. A senior pastor or minister of discipleship should provide this type of leadership, of course. Yet many of them in family-based churches view what happens with families as the concern of the children's minister or the youth pastor. Family-based churches must spend some real time considering how their vision for connecting families can be developed churchwide, and how staff members will be held accountable. In family-equipping churches, every aspect in every ministry is coordinated around a shared vision that calls every minister to equip parents to become primary disciple-makers in their children's lives. In our particular congregation, our structure as an emerging generations team with a clear leader facilitates this type of strategic planning.

In family-based churches, there is also a danger in taking a "shotgun" approach to parent ministry. What I mean by that is that it is easy to scatter a lot of opportunities for parents throughout existing ministry structures and calendars—say a mother-daughter event here, a few weeks of father-son interaction there, a family camp or mission trip in another open slot. Yet, if we plan to equip parents properly, it is going to require *strategic movement* through a specific series of intentionally planned steps that helps parents at every level of understanding. From parents who are not yet believers to parents who are strong believers trying to choose a family mission project or wondering how best to lead family worship, there must be carefully planned and communicated steps throughout our strategy. Just as we only have a few years with children and students, we only have a few years with parents in which to make a difference; thus, we must use our time wisely. A rifle with a laser sight is much more accurate over a longer distance because it is focused. Ministry to parents needs to be approached in the same way.

Finally, many family-based churches have a tendency to hold on to the idea that ministry events are what have the greatest significant spiritual impact on teenagers' lives. Admittedly, even in family-equipping churches, events *do* have a place. In some cases events serve as catalysts to introduce new students to a ministry or to call current students to renew their commitments. The role of events should, however, be limited and carefully coordinated within the entire scope of ministry. Otherwise students become spiritually codependent on emotional moments that occur apart from the day-by-day disciplines of life. In the process students fail to develop a truly biblical framework that calls for a lifestyle of worship (Rom 12:1–2). Instead, they become "worship junkies" looking for that next "camp spiritual high."[10] Yet the experiences having the greatest lifelong impressions on children and students are not high-intensity events. According to findings cited by Richard Ross, the deepest impressions on students' lives occur in far more mundane contexts, such as serving alongside parents in ministry or mission settings.[11]

Like the family-based model, the family-equipping model features flexibility, balance, and a capacity to show Christian compassion to all sorts of people. Unlike the family-based model, family-equipping ministry restructures all the church's ministries to offer a comprehensive, overarching vision for families that extends from preschool through college years.

In the family-equipping model, no individual student pastor or children's minister bears the weight of equipping parents. The family-equipping approach calls everyone to work together, holding every staff member accountable to equip families to function as contexts for discipleship. Every ministry shares in the church-home partnership, recognizing that this partnership is not simply one more fad or trend to come from the age-graded world of ministry. In the family-equipping congregation, this partnership between church and home is central to our identity.

---

10. See *Toxic Faith* by Stephen Arterburn and Jack Felton (New York: Random House, 2001) for an in-depth look at how a dependence on emotional religious experience can follow the same pattern as addiction.

11. Quoted by Dr. Richard Ross, based on his research at Southwestern Seminary, during the Turning Hearts Tour in 2006.

# Why Family-Based Ministry Still Works

*Brandon Shields*

First of all, I thank the other contributors for their concerns, critiques, and encouragement of the family-based model. As a continual learner, I hope I will always welcome criticism and learn from the ways others pursue Jesus' mission of advancing His kingdom through the local church. I will strive to do that. At the same time, I remain convinced that the family-based model is best positioned to address the real challenges facing today's young people and their families. My hope is that church leaders would look past the clever rhetoric and alarmist statistical hype that has punctuated much of this discussion. When we take a fresh look at the facts, the family-based model still stands as the approach providing every family with the best possible opportunity to experience the life-changing power of the gospel.

## Family-Based Ministry and Sola Scriptura

Let me be clear from the get-go that I affirm wholeheartedly the concept of *sola Scriptura* in the life, mission, and practice of the local church. Furthermore, I believe that family-based models—as well as family-integrated and family-equipping models—can serve as biblically based paradigms for pursuing ministry to the church's families. While the structures are radically divergent, each model articulated in these pages strives to begin with Scripture as the rule and standard for the church's mission and practices. Even though all three models can serve as biblically based paradigms, I see too many weaknesses in the family-integrated and family-equipping approaches to embrace either perspective.

The proponent of the family-integrated model has, unfortunately, couched his disagreement with family-based ministry in terms of an oversimplified dichotomy between "biblical" and "unbiblical." This is typical of those who hold to extreme perspectives on the regulative principle: Only elements, forms, and traditions clearly stated in the Bible are appropriate for the contemporary church. Pursuing this strategy, the author then demonizes the family-based model as a *sola cultura* approach.

Once again, I admit that there is no clear biblical mandate—that is to say, no specific command in the biblical text explicitly calling every church to embrace the family-based model of ministry. This does not lead to the conclusion, however, that this model is unbiblical or that family-based churches do not subscribe to *sola Scriptura*. Biblical fidelity means that churches articulate and apply broad biblical and theological principles as the absolute interpretive grid by which every philosophy, teaching, leadership structure, ministry offering, and decision is judged. Where certain marks of the church are biblically mandated, such as preaching, church discipline, or the exercise of the ordinances, churches are bound to organize themselves accordingly. Where the Scripture is silent, however, churches are free to pursue culturally appropriate methods for carrying out their mission to evangelize the lost and to disciple the saints. Edmund Clowney puts it like this:

> The New Testament gives us principles, not an order of service or detailed directions for conducting worship. . . . He had given some specific instructions . . . but his general command indicates that they are free to arrange the circumstances of worship in a respectable and orderly way.[12]

---

12. E. Clowney, *The Church: Contours of Christian Theology* (Downers Grove, Ill.: InterVarsity Press, 1995), 126.

The Westminster Confession speaks to this same issue of freedom in ecclesiastical organization:

> There are some circumstances concerning the worship of God, and government of the Church, common to human actions and societies, which are to be ordered by the light of nature, and Christian prudence, according to the general rules of the Word, which are always to be observed.[13]

In other words, necessary contextualizations will be taking place as the gospel takes root in various cultures. Certain cultural realities have always driven the church to reconsider her own traditions and methods in order to separate what is biblically indispensable from peripheral traditions that might pose unnecessary obstacles to the spreading of the gospel. The accounts found in the sixth and fifteenth chapters of Acts stand as examples of this process, even in the first few years of the church's existence.

My point is that all churches make contextual decisions, within biblical parameters, to determine the best way to reach the lost culture in which God has placed them. Our particular family-based church proclaims the gospel in English, uses Western architecture and engineering methods, podcasts sermons, and organizes ministries in age-appropriate ways—all to the glory of God and for the advancement of God's kingdom through Jesus Christ. Where are we being biblically unfaithful?

In fact, in the family-based church, our insistence on *sola Scriptura* is part of what fuels our ministry paradigms. It is precisely because I believe in the real existence of hell, as presented in Scripture, that I preach the gospel weekly to hundreds of unsaved teenagers in my family-based congregation. It is because of the Great Commission given in Scripture that I work to make disciples by identifying age-appropriate structures and teaching methods. Because I believe wholeheartedly in the command of Jesus in Scripture to embrace "the little children"—those that others would ignore—I serve as a youth pastor in a family-based church.

---

13. Ibid., 126–27.

Children and young people remain the greatest hope for the gospel in the world. Statistically, they are the largest people group, and they represent the most receptive demographic to the Christian message. Shame on us as a church if we do not share the heart of Jesus for children in the way we structure our resources, ministries, and evangelistic efforts! Such clear missiological need demands a clear missiological response from the church.

## Intentionality in the Evangelization of Children and Youth

The clearest line of demarcation between family-based strategies and the other options presented in this book is the intentionality of efforts to reach lost young people. Perhaps the proponent of family-integrated ministry stated it best when he criticized the family-based model for engaging in "evangelism that focuses primarily on children and youth." But I don't see that as a problem. I take it as a compliment. In fact, I would argue that the evangelization of children and youth has been and always should be an imminent priority in the church.

Jonathan Edwards, describing the revival that he witnessed in the eighteenth century, commented,

> The work has been chiefly amongst the young; and comparatively but few others have been made partakers of it. And indeed it has commonly been so, when God has begun any great work for the revival of his church; he has taken the young people, and has cast off the old and stiff-necked generation.[14]

Edwards's observation concerning young people's receptivity to the gospel became a hallmark in the ministries of other pastors and revivalists, including Charles G. Finney, Dwight L. Moody, John Wesley, and Charles Spurgeon. Addressing the need to focus evangelistic efforts toward the young, Spurgeon wrote:

> If we are to be a blessing to them, they must lie in our hearts—they must be our daily and nightly charge. We must

---

14. A. Reid, *Introduction to Evangelism* (Nashville, Tenn.: B&H, 1998), 255–56.

take the cases of our children to our silent couch with us: we must think of them in the watches of the night, and when we cannot sleep because of care, they must share in those midnight anxieties. . . . We must not place the child far from us, out of doors, or down below us in a vault of cold forgetfulness, but, if we would have him raised to life, we must place him in the warmest sympathies of our hearts.[15]

In an ideal scenario, perhaps we would put fathers in the crosshairs of our evangelistic efforts. Yet we must acknowledge that a growing segment of teenagers simply do not enjoy the familial luxury of a father in the home. Millions of lost, hurting, and confused teenagers litter a landscape of broken marriages throughout North America. Can we be content responding merely by pouring more resources into programs and structures that cater to intact families?

The more we focus on reaching young people as a distinguishable group, the more we will witness revival in our churches. We must go where they are, preach to them in their language, compel them to come to Jesus, and consistently create attractive environments where persons from any background can grow in their relationship with Jesus. These missiological convictions are the fuel that drives the engine of family-based ministry.

## Strategic Balance and Intentionality

Proponents of other family ministry models have expressed concern that family-based ministry does not go far enough in strategically encouraging parents to serve as the primary disciplemakers of their children.

Let me say a few things about this. First, each age-organized ministry exists as one piece of the family-based church's discipleship mechanism. Intentional training of families to become contexts for discipleship happens every day in a number of different ways, such as midweek men's and women's small groups, marriage retreats, breakfast meetings with leadership teams, Sunday

---

15. Charles Spurgeon, *The Soul Winner* (Grand Rapids, Mich.: Eerdmans, 1994), 151.

morning preaching, the pastor's Bible study with the men, and a myriad of other gatherings. The best training for family discipleship happens when churches invest time and energy into building up marriages. As parents learn to love each other as Jesus loved the church, the entire family unit is transformed, and family discipleship is a natural outflow.

The most effective family training will not occur primarily at a youth event under the supervision of the student ministry team. Yet the critical component to ensuring proper discipleship in a family-based church is collaboration where everyone working together multiplies the effectiveness of each person and group. Such collaboration is not limited to small churches or to integrated ministry structures. It can happen in larger congregations, too. It is not a matter of *structure* but of *intentionality*. The family-equipping movement seems to get this; family-integrated churches do not.

The real genius of the family-based approach is *strategic balance*. From my perspective, both of the other models put forth in this book lean too far toward catering their ministries to intact families. I am not comfortable with any model of ministry where the primary strategic question is, Is this God's best for families? Such a question excludes God's best for those outside the faith-community or whose families are shattered and fragmented. Proponents of family-integrated ministry take this attitude one step further and suggest that they do not evangelize youth and children directly, seeking instead to evangelize families.

In the family-based approach, youth pastors have the time and resources to focus on directly engaging the youth culture with the gospel. In addition, family-based churches have the flexibility to offer coordinated and diverse curricula to train parents to disciple their children, resulting in a synergy of evangelism and discipleship that spreads throughout the congregation.

## The Family-Based Approach: Common-Sense Realism

In the final analysis, I think something much simpler will drive most churches to embrace a family-based paradigm over the other two options: *common-sense realism*. What I mean by this is viewing the world as it is. No candy coating. No pie-in-the-sky theology. We take people and culture as they are before attempting to impose our idealistic visions on them.

Common-sense realism reveals that we live in a culture where millions of young people do not know Jesus. Marriages and families are crumbling as the effects of divorce and sexual immorality cripple everyone involved. In the shadow of these struggles, the family-based approach provides a biblically based, strategically balanced, practically applicable model for ministry. Any church, of any size, with any community demographic, can adapt these ideas with the hope of long-term success bringing honor to Jesus and producing the strongest families. That is the sort of ministry paradigm that makes the most sense to me.

CHAPTER 9

# Family-Equipping Ministry
CHURCH AND HOME AS COCHAMPIONS
## Jay Strother

*Minister to Emerging Generations*
*Brentwood Baptist Church*
*Brentwood, Tennessee*

John Kotter's best-selling book *Our Iceberg Is Melting* introduces us to a fable about a colony of emperor penguins living in Antarctica. The catalytic character is a penguin named Fred. Fred is an "unusually curious and observant" emperor penguin. Fred's research has led him to an alarming conclusion: The iceberg that he knows as his home—the very iceberg that, according to his fellow penguins, "will always be our home"—is cracking. Soon, it might even break into pieces. Fred doesn't panic easily, but the more he ponders their situation, the more he becomes unnerved.

Despite the fact that he isn't a senior leader in the penguin community, Fred "knows he has to do something." His convictions lead him to inform key leaders about the issue. Perhaps most important, he shows them the problem in ways that lead beyond conflict to community consensus.[1]

Fred's iceberg is not the only context cracking right now. There are cracks in the iceberg we know as the contemporary church, especially when it comes to ministries to children and

---

1. Summarized from J. Kotter and H. Rathgeber, *Our Iceberg Is Melting: Changing and Succeeding Under Any Conditions* (New York: St. Martin's, 2005).

students. Some have denied that there are any cracks in the iceberg at all. Others act as if the iceberg has already shattered, and the church is adrift in a frigid sea. I and other proponents of family-equipping ministry think the time is right to follow Fred's lead and move toward constructive consensus and lasting solutions.

## The Cracks in Our Iceberg

In the past several years, more than a few Christian leaders have noticed significant "cracks" in our ministry contexts. Their love for the church and their concern for future generations led them to make some important observations regarding these cracks, and I wish to highlight some of them to show ways that lead to better models for ministry.

One of the primary cracks in our iceberg has a name: *moral therapeutic deism*. In 2005, sociologist Christian Smith coined this phrase to describe the core religious values held by the overwhelming majority of American teenagers, not only those outside the church but also those raised in the church.

Summing up four years of research for the National Study of Youth and Religion, Smith's analysis of moral therapeutic deism provided a definition for something that has been a growing concern among persons working with children and youth: *Despite strong interest in religion and even active participation in vibrant churches, millions of students in our ministries were unable to articulate even the most basic tenets of Christian faith*. Young people are emerging from our children's ministries and youth programs with the belief that religion is all about doing better and becoming happier; for the most part they perceive God as a distant and benign Creator whose purpose is largely to help us feel better about ourselves.[2] Despite all the investments and supposed advances in age-organized ministries over the past thirty years, churched children and youth are growing up less likely than ever before to have a biblical perspective on life.

---

2. Smith and Denton, *Soul Searching* (see chap. 5, n. 101).

## Becoming "Freds"

A few years ago our church developed a ministry team to see how these trends were impacting our students. Despite having worked to refocus our ministries to meet students' spiritual needs and their evangelistic drive, we still seemed to be hitting an invisible wall. The church had creativity, resources, and highly trained leadership—everything that seemed necessary to make a lasting impact in the lives of children and teenagers. And so many good things *had* happened. We had moved light-years forward from the days when youth ministers flipped through clip-art books, trying to come up with activities to entertain a handful of middle-school boys.

Yet something wasn't right.

It seemed as if each question about ministry led to another question, then another and another, a process we compared to "peeling an onion." Why did most of our students struggle to live their faith in their everyday life? Why was it difficult for them to hold on to any biblical truth deeper than what could be phrased on a camp T-shirt or bumper sticker? Why did so many young ladies and young men have serious inner spiritual identity issues that led to difficulties with diets, dress, and dating?

A difficult but obvious truth finally dawned on us: These were the same issues their parents were dealing with, struggles with deeper faith, authentic spirituality, and Christ-centered identity. In fact, one father had recently criticized a team member for encouraging his daughter to "read her Bible too much" and to become "too spiritual for her own good." There was a gap between the church's ideals and parents' actual practices and expectations.

As we examined our context, here is what we concluded: In our well-intentioned efforts to reach students for Jesus Christ, we had developed ministry models failing to call parents to embrace their role as primary disciple-makers in their children's lives. The church had tacitly encouraged this parental abdication by relentlessly promoting benefits and life changes that would accompany increased participation in ministry activities. As a result, the church and families were being split spiritually along too many key fault lines.

In the midst of this reassessment, God convicted us of a simple truth: *The home has the greatest impact on young lives; with few exceptions, if we fail to impact the home, we will never make a lasting impact on students.* Thus far, we had relied on traditional models of youth and children's ministry. But these models were insufficient to meet this generation's spiritual needs. At best, these models for children's and youth ministry gave only the slightest nod to the parents, the vital people God designed to nurture young faith, day in and day out. At worst, these past models ignored parents or even worked against them.

The iceberg of ministry as we once knew it was cracking. Just as Fred the penguin looked carefully at his surroundings and concluded that cracks in the iceberg were threatening his colony, we saw that cracks between the church and the home were endangering the vitality of Christian faith in our congregation. Armed with these convictions, our team set out to be the "Freds" in our church. Our goal? To engage our church's leadership in a radical restructuring of priorities that would reengage parents in the spiritual lives of their youth and children.

## What Happens When Fred Comes to Church

How did we engage in this change process? For starters, we prayed and pondered where we were and where God wanted us to go. We listened to parents. We looked at the handful of other churches that seemed to see the same issues we had perceived. We listened to family ministry pioneers, and we considered what some of the latest research had highlighted—like the study from Barna Research that came to this conclusion:

> The ministries having the greatest success at seeing young people emerge into mature Christians, rather than contented churchgoers, are those that facilitate a parent-church partnership focused on instilling specific spiritual beliefs and practices in a child's life from a very early age.[3]

---

3. BarnaResearch, "SpiritualProgressHardtoFind:www.barna.org/FlexPage.aspx?Page =BarnaUpdate&BarnaUpdateID=155.

Most important of all, our team rediscovered a rich collection of biblical truths. These truths enabled us to articulate our growing conviction that the best path to impact future generations would require recovering the ancient path of spiritual formation that is built on the foundation of strong families and strong faith communities working together.

The practices we developed fit into a pattern of ministry that Timothy Paul Jones has dubbed "the family-equipping model." Family-equipping churches stand with family-integrated and family-based congregations in their call for parents to serve as primary disciple-makers in their children's lives.

So what makes a family-equipping church different from family-integrated or family-based congregations?

Unlike proponents of family-integrated ministry, family equippers do not call for complete abolition of all age-organized ministries. In family-equipping churches one is likely to find some youth and children's programs or activities. At the same time, family-equipping ministries place a far higher premium on intergenerational interaction than the typical family-based church. Unlike family-based churches, family-equipping congregations do not believe it is enough merely to tweak or refocus existing youth and children's programs. We see serious, systemic problems in present practices of ministry. As a result, the iceberg is cracking. The cracks in the iceberg demand radical reconstructions to remold and rework entire organizational structures in the church. Such reconstructions are necessary for parents and churches to walk the ancient paths of Christian formation as cochampions with a single goal.[4]

**What's Distinctive about a "Family-Equipping Church"?**

Family-equipping churches retain some age-organized ministries but restructure the congregation to partner with parents at every level of ministry so that parents are acknowledged, equipped, and held accountable for the discipleship of their children.

4. Here, and throughout this chapter, the term *cochampion* alludes to Wright and Graves, *reThink* (see chap. 2, n. 28).

## Turning Churches and Families into Cochampions

For us, the process of reconstruction began by capturing a new term for what we were doing; our ministry became known as a ministry to "emerging generations." Both terms encapsulated important values: *Emerging* indicated that children and youth are not only the future of the church but also a vital part of the church's present life. Young believers are not just the church of tomorrow, they are also the church today, and they should be called to responsibility and maturity as full participants in our community of faith. (And for the record, the choice of this term "emerging generations" had *nothing* to do with the current "emergent" or even "emerging" movements in the church. That is another question entirely.)

*Generations* is a biblical term appearing throughout Scripture more than 150 times in the Old Testament (the Hebrew word is *dor*) and nearly five dozen times in the New Testament (the Greek words are *genea* and *genos*). For us, this term emphasizes the permanence that spiritual formation can have when it is rooted in parents' discipleship of their children. Our goal is to partner with parents to raise not just a youth group but a generation that loves God with heart, soul, mind, and strength (Mark 12:28–34).

## Engaging and Equipping, Partnering and Planning

The emerging generations team rallied around the idea of synchronizing and restructuring every age-organized ministry around the focus of partnering with parents. This team embraced a specific responsibility for charting the congregation's course in two key areas. The first was engaging and equipping parents as their children's primary disciplers, and the second one was partnering with parents to develop a definite plan for their children's Christian formation.

### Engaging and Equipping Parents

How did we pursue the first responsibility of engaging and equipping parents to serve as primary disciple-makers in their children's lives? Like many other thriving North American churches, we long ago adopted an age-organized approach that separated different generations from one another in almost every area of ministry. From the standpoint of numbers, this approach had been highly successful. One unintended consequence of this approach was a series of isolated ministry "silos"—or, as it has been described in an earlier chapter, "an octopus without a brain." Members from one generation rarely saw members of another generation, and different generations certainly were not growing together spiritually. In some cases, ministries to different age groups were competing with one another for space, resources, and attention.

Worse yet, it was painfully apparent that parents had abdicated the responsibility for their children's discipleship. In our pride, we had been glad to indulge this abdication with an ever-expanding and always dazzling array of programs for youth and children. But it quickly became clear that if we intended parents to become the primary spiritual catalysts in their children's lives instead of relying on the church's programs, we would need to restructure our entire approach to ministry.

### Partnering for Growth

The second responsibility for the emerging generations team was to partner with parents to develop a comprehensive vision for their children's spiritual formation. Here is why this responsibility was so important: Over time it became clear that it was not enough to have excellent preschool, children, student, and collegiate ministries. Those ministries had to agree on key philosophies, and at the core of these key philosophies was the recognition of the family as the context where foundations of faith should be formed.

The essential thing became the simple recognition that God ordained two institutions to form the spiritual lives of emerging generations—the family and the church. The development of spiritual maturity in children's lives would require a carefully planned partnership between these two institutions. With that recognition, we drew our line in the sand and determined to champion both institutions in every ministry, regardless of the cost.

## Discipleship through Partnership

As we worked with parents instead of without them or even against them, it became apparent we had overlooked an obvious early step. In the early days of planning, we assumed that pretty much every parent would agree with us when it came to our purpose and expectations for their children's spiritual development.

We were wrong.

As it turned out, most parents *did* have a purpose for their children's lives, but this purpose was *not* maturity in Jesus Christ. Their purpose was for their children to be "happy." And what exactly was necessary for their children to achieve this elusive goal? To enable their children to attain happiness, parents in our community tended to push their children into high-stress combinations of college preparatory courses, extracurricular activities, and specialized sports programs. The parents' driving assumption was that these experiences were essential for their children to get into good colleges, which would result in good jobs, which would enable the children to achieve the same high standards of material living as their parents, which would in turn make the children—you guessed it, *happy.*

What these parents did not know is that these same students walked into our offices or met us at coffee shops to tell us, "My parents are rich, important, successful—and miserable. I don't want their life. Help me find something better!" There's a paradox at work here because these children enjoyed the material comforts their parents' lifestyle provided, and yet these same young people also saw through the veneer of their parents' false and fleeting values.

While higher education and productive careers do have their place, Scripture presents a far higher goal for child-rearing than the formation of well-educated or well-paid adults. "The vision for the next generation," Richard Ross and Ken Hemphill point out, "should be nothing less than raising them with the conviction that their primary goal is to leverage their lives to advance God's kingdom so that every tribe, nation and people group have the opportunity to respond to their rightful king."[5]

What we discovered was that most parents, even Christian parents, would "default" to the world's definitions of happiness and success in parenting unless we consistently placed a biblical understanding of their responsibilities in front of them. Children are gifts from God, given to parents to be equipped for His purposes. Yet, because most parents in our churches were never discipled by their own parents, these parents did not naturally arrive at biblical conclusions about their responsibilities. To impact the emerging generations, we had to guide parents to a simple but critical conclusion about our ministry, that *our ultimate goal is to bring the home and the church together in a biblical partnership to raise up a generation that loves God and loves others.* In the simplest possible terms, our goal became discipleship through partnership.

## Planning to Reach the Right Goal

Of course it is one thing to have a great goal in mind but quite another to build a ministry plan that moves you toward that goal. On the heels of praying, planning, listening, and learning, we developed a plan we called a "Spiritual Formation Model for Emerging Generations" to move us toward our goal of discipleship through partnership with parents.

In developing this model, the emerging generations team researched and identified three primary areas of lasting influence on children's spiritual development. The team summarized these three areas in three crucial words: *catalysts, content,* and *context*. Let's look at each of these terms together to understand how it is possible to partner with parents in the spiritual formation of their children.

---

5. K. Hemphill and R. Ross, *Parenting with Kingdom Purpose* (Nashville, Tenn.: B&H, 2005), 7.

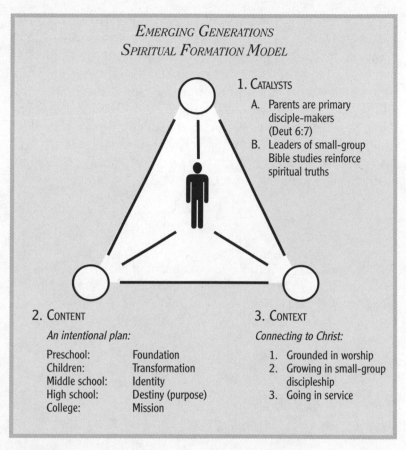

EMERGING GENERATIONS
SPIRITUAL FORMATION MODEL

1. CATALYSTS

A. Parents are primary disciple-makers (Deut 6:7)
B. Leaders of small-group Bible studies reinforce spiritual truths

2. CONTENT

*An intentional plan:*

| | |
|---|---|
| Preschool: | Foundation |
| Children: | Transformation |
| Middle school: | Identity |
| High school: | Destiny (purpose) |
| College: | Mission |

3. CONTEXT

*Connecting to Christ:*

1. Grounded in worship
2. Growing in small-group discipleship
3. Going in service

## Catalysts

God designed parents to serve as primary spiritual catalysts in their children's lives. Research shows that even active students receive only forty hours or so of biblical instruction each year from their churches. Parents, on the other hand, have more than three thousand hours a year in which they are constantly "teaching" their children in some way![6] We recognized that if we wanted to see an emerging generation that loves God with everything in them, we would have to redirect our ministry's time and energies toward equipping parents to impress truth in their children's lives day by day.

---

6. R. Joiner, "Clearing Up Family Ministry Confusion": www.orangeleaders.com.

From this point every family-equipping church's plan will look a little different. In our particular congregation the plan to equip parents became known as *Parenting 6.7*. This title pointed parents to Deut 6:7, the touchstone text for our ministry: "Repeat [these words] to your children. Talk about them when you sit in your house and when you walk along the road, when you lie down and when you get up." It also reminded parents and leaders of the inner workings of our plan. The plan required parents and leaders to work together to build *six biblical characteristics* into each child's life through *seven ministry strategies.*

---

*Deuteronomy 6:7*
*Ministry Plan*

*Our goal as a church is to partner with parents to see God raise up generations of children and students who love God with all their hearts, souls, and strength. We hope that our students and children will:*

**1** Love God as a way of life (worship). See Rom 12:1–2.

**2** Love others as a way of life (service). See Mark 10:45.

**3** Love the church and understand their roles in the body of Christ (community). See Eph 4:4–7.

**4** Love the Bible and can handle it properly as the authority and foundation for life (Scripture). See 2 Tim 3:15–17.

**5** Love to tell others about Christ (the gospel) and share their stories (testimony). See Rom 10:14–15.

**6** Love to grow closer to God through personal spiritual disciplines such as prayer and Bible study (discipleship). See 1 Tim 4:7–12.

---

The six biblical characteristics flesh out what it means to love God. They represent an irreducible minimum cluster of traits that are necessary for children and students to live lives of vibrant faith. The six characteristics call parents to partner with the church with the goal of training their children to love God as a way of life (Rom 12:1–2), to love others as a way of life (Mark 10:45), to love the church and to understand their role in the body of Christ (Eph 4:4–7), to love Scripture and to handle it properly as the authority and foundation for all of life (2 Tim 3:15–17), to love to tell others about Jesus Christ and to share their own story of faith (Rom 10:14–15), and to love to grow closer to God through personal spiritual disciplines (1 Tim 4:7–12).

In Deut 6:7, the Hebrew phrase translated "impress them on your children" or "repeat them to your children" uses *shanan*, an important Hebrew verb. The word *shanan* meant "to chisel in stone" or "to whet a blade"—actions implying repetitive, intentional, transformative activity. To chisel the six biblical characteristics into children's lives, the emerging generations team developed seven specific strategies for ministry:

1. **Ministry Strategy 1:** Synchronize all ministry efforts around the recognition that two partnered influences— church and home—have the greatest potential to impact young lives. Everything must be planned and viewed with families as a priority. In every planning and evaluation meeting, we challenge ourselves with this question: Is this God's best for families?

2. **Ministry Strategy 2:** Clearly communicate expectations and plans to parents. If parents are the primary disciple-makers, every ministry and leader exists to support but never to replace the parents' role. A key objective for the entire church is to "equip and support parents in making their homes ministry centers for the spiritual growth of their children." This message is communicated church-wide through every venue, all the way from Sunday sermons to the monthly coffee that's hosted for expectant mothers. We want them to get the message even before their baby is born!

3. **Ministry Strategy 3:** Develop a resource guide to recommend resources for family devotions and family issues.

An average of ten new parenting books have been published every *day* for the past twenty-one years—more than 75,000 books![7] Don't send your parents to a Christian bookstore or to do online shopping alone. Help them to wade through options to find the best biblically centered resources. This guide is posted on the church Web site, and it is available in printed form throughout the building.

4. **Ministry Strategy 4:** Connect the church's teaching ministries to the home. Before our transition to family-equipping partnerships, many parents had no clue who was teaching their child's Bible study or small group. Now, one goal in our team is for every group leader to call the parents of each child in their group in the first few weeks of the fall semester to say something like this: "Hi, I lead your son's LifeGroup. I want you to know that we're on the same team, and I support you as the parent. Here's what we'll be teaching this semester, and here is my contact information. Is there anything you want me to know about your son? How can I pray for him and your family right now?" This expectation works in every size ministry setting and is incredibly simple, yet it is a powerful way to reinforce the church-home partnership. The emerging generations team also intentionally selects Bible study materials with discussion pages that are sent home with children or made available online. These resources become vital tools to link what is taught at church with in-home spiritual conversations.

5. **Ministry Strategy 5:** Provide catalytic venues to introduce parents to the expectations of Parenting 6.7. If you have worked with parents in a church, you may already have observed an intriguing dynamic: The vast majority of parents who are attracted to parent-equipping opportunities are parents who already "get it"! So how can you introduce parents who don't "get it" to the value of a family-equipping partnership? For us, the answer be-

7. Barna, *Revolutionary Parenting*, xi (see chap. 4, n. 78).

came catalytic venues. On a regular basis, the church hosts a "Family Matters" luncheon immediately after morning worship services. During this catalytic venue, we focus on a specific topic that equips parents to become better disciple-makers in their children's lives. By connecting this catalytic venue to a Sunday worship celebration, there is a much greater rate of participation. Wednesday evenings became another catalytic venue. To equip parents who drop off their children for midweek programs—and, hopefully, to draw these parents toward a commitment to be more involved in their children's discipleship—we began to host equipping events for these parents at regular intervals. It is essential for all parents to be made aware of their responsibility and to be equipped to become the primary disciple-maker in their children's lives.

6. **Ministry Strategy 6:** Provide family-equipping mission opportunities. The spiritual activity that leaves the most significant lifelong impression on children and students is serving alongside their parents. That is why we prioritize opportunities for families to serve together inside and outside the church walls. Whether it is weekly in preschool, annually in preparing Thanksgiving food baskets, or a once-in-a-lifetime trip to repair homes in hurricane-ravaged communities on the Gulf Coast, we constantly look at every ministry and mission opportunity, asking, "How will families be involved in this?"

7. **Ministry Strategy 7:** Partner with the worship team to develop intergenerational and family worship gatherings. Children and students are an important part of the worshiping community! We are convinced that families are strengthened when the generations worship together, and that is why we offer opportunities like "Big Enough for Big Church" to teach our youngest worshipers and their parents why we worship in the way that we do. All through the year, we look for creative ways to connect the message shared in the worship center with children's

lives. At key moments each year, we even plan worship experiences specifically for families. For instance, on Easter Sunday, our church has overflow venues and multiple services because our main worship center simply cannot handle the crowds. Instead of having latecomers watch a video feed, we designed a family-friendly worship experience in the overflow venue that included pre-service stations where children tasted, touched, and felt elements from the drama of Holy Week. After that, families experienced a worship service led by our children's worship team and witnessed baptisms.

These seven strategies do not represent everything that might be done. In fact, they may not even be the strategies that we focus on forever. We want, as pastor and author Andy Stanley has put it, always to fall in love with a biblical vision but never to fall in love with a specific method.

Why such a short list of strategies? Why restructure all existing ministries? Why not simply add a ministry alongside all the other ministries to implement these strategies? This is why: It is tempting simply to define family ministry as adding more "stuff" for already busy families. Yet, if we multiply families' busyness by involving them in more church activities, families have less time to be together, and we defeat our entire purpose of calling parents to serve as day-by-day disciplers in their children's lives. That is why we limit ourselves to seven simple strategies instead of ever-increasing lists of events and programs.

As you can see, most of our ministry's efforts revolve around developing parents as disciple-makers. The rest of our energies are concentrated on equipping caring adult leaders—the second spiritual catalyst in the lives of children and students.

Some family ministry models completely eliminate formal, age-organized Bible studies with adult leaders apart from the parents. Our team remains convinced that adult leaders have crucial roles to play in children's spiritual development. Caring adult leaders can partner with parents to help children and youth root their emerging identities in Jesus Christ.

Another reason for developing caring adult leaders is that though intact Christian families represent God's perfect plan for his people, such systems have broken down for many children and teenagers. What is God's plan for millions of young people who have no committed parents? We believe God calls communities of believers to care for these "spiritual orphans" by surrounding them with caring adult believers who will share the hope of Christ while modeling what a Christian family ought to look like. When home structures break down, these meaningful relationships with caring adults have the greatest potential to provide children and youth with hope for a better future. According to a study conducted by Dartmouth Medical School that focused on at-risk adolescents,

> what really holds potential for making a moral impact on a mid-adolescent is a powerful connection with individual adults whom he can admire or idealize. It is the individual teacher, coach, counselor, religious youth worker, Big Brother, grandparent, or other individuals in the community who can inspire him to make moral sense of the social confusion of his surroundings.[8]

Even as adult leaders care for the needs of spiritual orphans, we maintain that the child's parents *ought to* be caring for those needs. That is why we encourage leaders to form relationships with every parent. The Christian warmth shown in these relationships challenges disconnected parents to reflect on what would motivate someone to care so deeply for their child or student. For many parents in our church, the journey to faith can be traced to the loving example of leaders who invested in their children.

## Content

We've looked carefully at the two catalytic influences in children's spiritual development, the church and the home. Now, let's look at the *content* that we provide to these catalysts. The

---

8. YMCA, Dartmouth Medical School, and the Institute of American Values, "Hardwired to Connect: The New Scientific Case for Authoritative Communities," in *A Report to the Nation from the Commission on Children at Risk,* 78: www.americanvalues.org.

emerging generations team does not assume that a particular publisher or curriculum company knows what our church needs. Instead, the team works strategically to design a scope and sequence of biblical principles that equip families and build family members from one age group to the next. The team then finds or creates resources to match that scope and sequence.

## Context

Since we have a limited amount of time with children and students, it is important for parents to know our "playbook"— to know what we expect the community of faith to accomplish in their children's lives. Reggie McNeil summarized the proper function of the community of faith with these words: "The community of faith should be an *environment* where the number one pursuit is the development of human beings created in the image of God and redeemed into his family through Jesus."[9] Almost every church would agree with this statement on paper. Yet we quickly discovered that, instead of strategizing contexts for spiritual development, we had in the past relied on programs and events that simply kept children and students busy. The majority of these programs and events did little to foster relational contexts that could develop disciples of Jesus Christ. What these programs and events actually did was create more consumers of church programs and services.

In light of this recognition, we began to view our ministry environments like a three-pronged electrical plug. We dubbed the three prongs *grounded, growing,* and *going.* Every ministry context should *ground* family members in worship, *grow* them in discipleship, and equip them to *go* on mission wherever God leads them.

In weekend worship whole families are *grounded* in a worship experience that brings multiple generations together. In midweek and weekend discipleship venues, caring leaders work to *grow* family members through biblical discussions that may be organized by age, life stage, or life circumstances. In all of

---

9. R. McNeil, *The Present-Future* (San Francisco, Calif.: Jossey-Bass, 2003), 91.

these environments, families receive encouragement to *go* to serve both locally and cross-culturally.

## Nothing New Under the Sun

This model of ministry is not supposed to be "new" or "cutting-edge." When God's people work faithfully to uncover the heart of the challenges facing their church, they discover there really is "nothing new under the sun" (Eccl 1:9)—and we have the wisest man who ever lived to back us up on that!

### For Generations to Come

In reclaiming the priority of family-equipping in our church, we are simply highlighting a theme that can be traced back to the Old Testament. In Genesis, Abraham received the promise of God's presence and of the possession of a permanent heritage. Even then the covenant was intended to be for future generations (Gen 17:8–9). Hundreds of years later, Moses made clear in the context of the faith community that parents in general, and fathers in particular, bore primary responsibility for their children's spiritual development and that the most critical truths about faith were "caught" as well as "taught" (Deut 6:4–9). The Passover, which is the central Old Testament feast, was a *family festival*. It was celebrated in the home, and the father presided over the meal (Exod 12:3,21).[10] Moses assumed that children would ask *their fathers* questions about the family's spiritual practices, and he commanded fathers to instruct them of the Lord's mighty saving deeds on behalf of his people (Exod 12:26–27; 13:13–15; Deut 6:20–25; Josh 4:5–7). Thus, according to the Old Testament, one of the main roles of the father, as the head of the home, was providing instruction for the spiritual development of his children.[11]

---

10. E. Sanchez, "Family in the Non-narrative Sections of the Pentateuch," in *Family in the Bible: Exploring Customs, Culture, and Context,* ed. Richard S. Hess and M. Daniel Carroll (Grand Rapids, Mich.: Baker, 2003), 41.

11. See C. Wright, *God's People in God's Land: Family, Land, and Property in the Old Testament* (Grand Rapids, Mich.: Eerdmans, 1990), 81–84; D. Block, "Marriage and Family in Ancient Israel," in *Marriage and Family in the Biblical World,* ed. K. Campbell (Downers Grove, Ill.: InterVarsity, 2003), 53; and P. Balla, *The Child-Parent Relationship in the New Testament and its Environment* (Peabody, Mass.: Hendrickson, 2003), 82.

The Bible is also brutally honest about what happens when parents abdicate their role as spiritual leaders in their homes. The book of Judges recounts the sad state of affairs that emerged when children were not raised to "know the LORD or the works He had done for Israel" (2:10–12; 1 Sam 2:12–3:14; 4:11–22; 8:1–9).

## The Best Small Group of All

"Teach a youth about the way he should go," the biblical sage declared to parents; "even when he is old he will not depart from it" (Prov 22:6).[12] Although children will receive some training in the context of the faith-community, it is virtually impossible to personalize teaching in corporate settings to develop every child in the right way. That is why the home was divinely designed to serve as the venue for that personalized level of discipleship.

The book of Proverbs is written from a father to his son, exhorting him to heed the spiritual guidance of his father and mother (Prov 1:8; 4:1–4; 6:20)—placing the primary locus of discipleship squarely within the family.[13] Over the past decades, many church-growth experts have concluded that the potential for life change is greatest in the intimacy and accountability of small discipleship groups. What is often missed is the fact that the family was the first and remains the best "small group" anywhere!

## Cochampioning Family and Faith Community in the New Testament

In Jewish communities of the first century AD, the home remained the central context for discipleship. At the same time, God designed people for relationships that extend far beyond the walls of believing homes. In the words of Jesus, "Whoever does the will of My Father in heaven, that person is My brother and sister and mother" (Matt 12:50). This recognition of believing relationships that reach beyond the home is why, in both Old and New Testaments, the greater community of faith supported the work begun in the home.

---

12. On this verse in particular and biblical parental instruction in Proverbs in general, see A. Köstenberger, *God, Marriage and Family: Rebuilding the Biblical Foundation* (Wheaton, Ill.: Crossway, 2004), 103–5 .

13. "In the Book of Proverbs," T. Longman III writes, "instruction takes place in a family setting" ("Family in the Wisdom Literature," in *Family in the Bible*, 84).

Jesus was raised not only in a faithful home but also within a faithful community, and both seem to have shaped his life. He possibly learned the Scriptures both from Joseph and in a local Jewish school or synagogue.[14] The fact is that Jesus' parents seem to have placed a great deal of personal confidence in the larger community! In the single biblical story that survives from the childhood of Jesus, his parents didn't even notice for an entire day's journey that he was not with them when they headed home from Jerusalem. They supposed their son to be somewhere "in the traveling party," the caravan of Jews traveling together toward Galilee (Luke 2:44). While parenting patterns are not the primary point of this text, it does appear that Joseph and Mary were apparently willing to entrust Jesus to caring adults in their community of faith.

Even at Pentecost, the importance of church-home partnership is apparent. When the Spirit's power grasped Simon Peter, the big fisherman made known that God's promise is "for you and for your children" (Acts 2:39). Believing households served as evangelistic outposts that impacted entire neighborhoods through hospitality and by serving as training centers for young leaders. When the head of a household was saved, the entire family often came to saving faith as well (e.g., Acts 11:14).

The New Testament affirms both the family's responsibility for the spiritual discipleship of children and the involvement of children in the faith community. Paul commands fathers to bring up their children "in the training and instruction of the Lord" (Eph 6:4). Timothy received biblical instruction and nurture from childhood from his mother and his grandmother (2 Tim 1:5; 3:14–15). Yet Paul also directly exhorted children themselves (Eph 6:1–3; Col 3:20). So, while parents are entrusted with the responsibility "of nurturing and cultivating a child's heart and mind in light of the Scriptures and

---

14. "In previous ages, formal education seems to have been exclusively the task of the father of the family. But by the first century, Jewish parents had schools available where reading and the Torah were taught" (Strange, *Children in the Early Church*, 13 [see chap. 2, n. 12]). See also the discussion of "Children in Jewish Culture and Society" in D. L. Stamps, "Children in Late Antiquity," in *Dictionary of New Testament Background*, ed. C. Evans and S. Porter (Downers Grove, Ill.: InterVarsity, 2000), 199–200.

on behalf of God,"[15] Paul's instructions specifically to children in his letters indicate that they "were taught and encouraged alongside the adults during the course of the church's meeting for worship."[16]

Even after the institutionalization of Christianity in the fourth century AD, multiple generations worshiped and served together in churches.[17] The Reformers and those who followed them emphasized the essential role of the family in the spiritual life of children. According to Martin Luther, since the father is responsible to instruct his children in godliness, he is "bishop and priest in his house."[18] The Puritans held family worship in high regard.[19] Two of the greatest preachers of any era, Jonathan Edwards and Charles Spurgeon, modeled their great concern for their own children's spiritual condition through regular leadership in family devotions.[20]

It has really been only in the past century or two, with the parachurch reactions that spawned age-specialized ministries both inside and outside the church, that church-home partnerships and intergenerational interaction gave way to discipleship programs that were generation specific and provided by professionals in isolation from the family. As a result of this societal shift, parents have increasingly abdicated their children's spiritual development or attempted to outsource their children's discipleship to ministry professionals. Reversing this trend will require a generation of convicted ministry leaders who see family-equipping as part of who they *are*—not as one more ministry that they *do*. Family-equipping ministry must begin to function as an integral lens bringing every aspect of the church's ministry into focus.

15. Köstenberger, *God, Marriage and Family*, 124–26.
16. Strange, *Children in the Early Church*, 74.
17. See, e.g., *Didascalia Apostolorum* 12.
18. M. Luther, "Lectures on Genesis: Chapters 21–25," in *Luther's Works* (55 vols.; trans. G. Schick; Saint Louis, Mo.: Concordia, 1964), 4:384.
19. H. Davies, *The Worship of the English Puritans* (repr., Morgan, Penn.: Soli Deo Gloria, 1997), 278–85.
20. See G. Marsden: *Jonathan Edwards: A Life* (New Haven, Conn.: Yale University, 2003), 321, and A. Dallimore, *Spurgeon: A New Biography* (Edinburgh, Scotland: Banner of Truth Trust, 1985), 178–79.

## Foundations for Implementing Family-Equipping Ministry

### Shared Priority Presented to the Parents

In order to develop an effective family-equipping ministry, a few foundational elements must be in place. In the first place, co-championing church and family cannot merely be a preference for your church; family-equipping ministry must represent the congregations's convictions about the entire nature of church and ministry. This priority does not occur automatically; it requires time and intentionality. Before our church made family-equipping a priority, we asked a group of parents, "What is the overall goal of our ministries to children and youth?" Their answers included *providing a safe place for kids, providing good activities for children while parents learn and worship, teaching kids that church is fun*, and *making disciples of students*. Only a few answers had anything to do with families.

Now I suspect the answers to that question would be radically different. We have placed a churchwide priority on *equipping and supporting parents in making their home the center for their children's spiritual growth*. By casting this as a churchwide priority, we have made clear that the church-home partnership is a process that extends beyond preschool, children's, or student ministry. The entire congregation shares ownership for the family-equipping ministry and bears the responsibility for implementation.

### Shared Practices Promoted through Proclamation

Priorities alone are not enough, though. Renewed organizational structures are needed to transform priorities into practices that impact the entire church culture. In our congregation this required restructuring of ministries from birth through college under a single ministry team—the emerging generations team. Instead of adding a "family minister" as one voice on a larger team, the church empowered the minister to emerging generations to champion the family in every context. As the minister to emerging generations, I am privileged to preach sermon series on the family, to share our vision with the senior leadership team, and to make certain that every small group understands the importance of church-home partnership. In all of these contexts, I constantly repeat the same message in different forms: *Parents are the primary disciple-makers in their children's lives.*

### Shared Perspective Prioritized among Staff Members

Every member of your ministerial team must align himself or herself with the priority of cochampioning church and home. This is more difficult than it sounds! Every team member must learn to view every area of responsibility through the same lens: What will best equip families to become the primary locus for children's spiritual formation? This question will challenge the ministry models that many staff members have employed in the past—models that may have been popular and even successful. Yet every goal, calendar, budget item, and space allocation must be coordinated to prioritize equipping parents and reducing stress on families. Unless every staff member works together to cochampion church and home, the vision for family ministry will break down at precisely the point that it needs to break through: in one's week-by-week ministry plan. Each team member's concern for the emerging generations must be greater than any desire to be seen as popular or successful in a particular area of ministry.

## Roadblocks on the Pathway to Family-Equipping Ministry

### The Spiritual Roadblock

Even after priorities, practices, and staffing have been aligned, the establishment of family-equipping ministry in the church will not be easy! In the first place, most church cultures are entrenched in traditions that have championed isolated age-organized programs instead of cochampioning the church-home partnership. But the struggle is not just against tradition; it is against a powerful, spiritual Enemy. One of this Enemy's greatest victories has been the systematic dissolution of the traditional family. Any attempt to reclaim families for God's kingdom will be met with spiritual opposition. That is why everything that is undertaken must be saturated in prayer and spiritual passion. A ministry team must be convinced and convicted that this is a hill that is, for the sake of the emerging generations, worth dying on.

## The Organizational Roadblock

Some resistance is not directly spiritual but rather results from organizational habits developed over decades in a congregation. The reason is that churches in North America have developed ministry structures that have imposed a business model on the church of Jesus Christ. In that model the pastor functions as a CEO, and ministry professionals or key leaders in the church do the work of ministry. The natural result of such a model is that people who attend such churches see themselves not as disciple-makers but as consumers of spiritual services that ministry professionals are responsible to provide.

Now for a moment of painful honesty. Many ministers thrive on this model not only because it is all they have ever known but also because it is how they receive validation and value. Parents and church members shower us with compliments for the hard work of leading, teaching, entertaining, and discipling children and students. We respond by working harder and harder until we are burned out. And why do we burn out? Because it is simply not possible for any ministry professional to do all that is required to disciple the church's children and students. I often point out to my leadership team that Jesus developed a dozen leaders, and one of those twelve went astray. If I think I can effectively develop more people than the Son of God, I am only fooling myself.

What is the solution?

It begins with the recovery of a biblical understanding of church leadership, that pastors and ministers are responsible to equip the saints to do the ministry. What this means in the context of family ministry is that the vocational minister's role is not to disciple children for their parents but to equip parents to disciple their own children. This biblical model will challenge every person on the team to reevaluate how they focus their time and priorities.

|  | Business Worldview* | Biblical Worldview |
|---|---|---|
| **Role of senior pastor** | CEO | Servant of the Word and equipper of the saints (Acts 6) |
| **Role of vocational ministers** | Hired professionals who do ministry | Equippers who train church members to do ministry (Eph 4) |
| **Role of members** | Consumers | Ministers and missionaries |
| **Role of parents** | Relinquish their spiritual role to paid professionals | Disciple their children, recognizing parents as the primary spiritual catalysts and disciple-makers in their children's lives |

\* Special thanks to Leon Drennen, a trustee of Brentwood Baptist Church and leader in the Nashville business community, for sharing this model.

## The Roadblock of Time

The family-equipping model requires years to take root and permeate every level of church life. Churches have not arrived at their current positions overnight, and they will not recover overnight either.

The forces of evil know well how incrementalism works, changing people's values little by little over decades. Think of how popular entertainment has gradually eroded Christian morals throughout the past century. The contemporary church does not seem to understand the value of incrementalism, though. Churches celebrate the momentary flash-bang of events that draw large crowds and lots of attention for a few moments, while ignoring the value of well-informed and well-planned steps that will impact families for generations. As one leadership maxim puts it, we overestimate what we can do in one year, but we underestimate what we can do in ten. Few churches have any clue what their ministry vision even looked like a decade ago, and perhaps very few ministers stick around in one church for that long! Yet family-equipping ministry is not a short-term fix. In order to take root and to flourish, this model requires long-term commitments from staff members and volunteers.

### The Programmatic Roadblock

Family-equipping ministry cannot be one more addition to the church's ever-expanding roster of programs. A church's long-term momentum will be killed if the impression is given that this is one more program for families to undertake and for church leaders to support. The purpose of family-equipping ministry is to change the way parents perceive parenting and to transform the entire discipleship process. That cannot be accomplished by adding one more program. It is only accomplished by carefully restructuring and redirecting the entire church.

## How Family-Equipping Works—and Why

James and Beth are the parents of ten-year-old Andrew. Typical of many parents in our area, James and Beth planned to connect with a church because they wanted Andrew to be a well-rounded child. For them, that meant raising their child in church, but they had no idea where to start. Their parents had taken them to church occasionally, and they had both professed faith in Jesus Christ. Yet they were clueless when it came to talking to Andrew about faith. There were also other issues, including the pressures of life revealing some serious fissures in their relationship after fifteen years of marriage.

Then a friend on Andrew's baseball team invited him to attend a children's Bible study. So one weekend two summers ago they attended church. In the worship service James and Beth were surprised to hear a message aimed at families. They had never recognized that God has called parents to be the primary spiritual catalysts in the lives of their children.

As James and Beth attended more regularly, they noticed their son came home each Sunday with a take-home guide that provided questions and suggestions for a time of family worship. They decided that each Sunday afternoon they would talk about what they learned in church and then pray together each night as Andrew went to bed.

A few weeks later the church hosted a "Family Matters" luncheon on the topic of healthy boundaries. Andrew's friends were playing online computer games, and Andrew had been begging for more "screen time." James and Beth showed up at the luncheon to get some practical advice about how to maintain healthy boundaries when it came to the computer. One couple at the luncheon invited James and Beth to join a new small group. There they studied the Scriptures and got to know other couples.

One week a couple in the small group shared how the church's missions and children's ministries were cosponsoring a mission trip for families. This trip would take families to the Gulf Coast to repair homes damaged by a hurricane. Such an expedition intrigued James and Beth, but they couldn't afford two summer trips. After some lengthy discussion, they gave up their yearly beach vacation and made their way to a small Mississippi town to repair hurricane-ravaged homes.

Alongside a dozen other families, they rebuilt a wheelchair ramp and reroofed an elderly couple's home. Each afternoon they helped lead a vacation Bible school in a local park. Before the week began, the parents had been trained not to jump in or to run everything but to encourage their children to lead. James and Beth were amazed when they watched their son plan, organize, and lead games for the children in this community! On the final evening Andrew told his parents that he had never personally trusted in Jesus Christ. James and Beth, moved by their son's openness, renewed their commitments to follow Jesus that night.

When the family returned home, Andrew attended a children's new Christian class with his parents, as required by the children's ministry staff. There church leaders equipped the family to talk about baptism, to engage in spiritual disciplines together, and to serve the church and the world. This past fall they made a family decision to attend worship services together as a family and to serve in a ministry that welcomes homeless men to church during winter months.

This is a real example of how a family-equipping ministry co-champions the church and the home. To be sure, this is not the story of every family in our church, but it demonstrates why we are convinced that the family-equipping model works.

The family-equipping model clearly communicates the value of the family at every level of church life. Wherever James and Beth went in our church, they simply could not avoid hearing the message that their role is not just to take their son to church but to serve as the primary spiritual catalyst in his life. At the same time, Andrew and his parents were introduced to the church through a dynamic children's ministry. While the pendulum in most churches has swung too far in the direction of professionalized ministers replacing parents as primary disciple-makers, swinging the pendulum too far in the opposite direction so that parents become the sole disciple-makers in a child's life is an equal and opposite mistake.

The family-equipping model allowed us to restructure existing age-organized ministries to champion the parent's role. By saying yes to this model, we intentionally say no to all other trends and agendas that might distract us from partnering with parents to raise a generation that loves God and loves others. The success of such a ministry cannot be measured by the number of children and students who participate in the ministry this week or next week. It is measured by the number whose experiences at home and in church impress the truth of Jesus Christ so deeply within them that they naturally train the next generation to live this same truth, talking about God's Word when they sit and when they walk, when they lie down and when they get up (Deut 6:7). Our vision is that children and students would "emerge" from families and ministries voicing their beliefs as clearly as David did:

> God, You have taught me from my youth,
> and I still proclaim Your wonderful works.
> Even when I am old and gray,
> God, do not abandon me.
> Then I will proclaim Your power to another generation,
> Your strength to all who are to come. (Ps 71:17–18)

CHAPTER 10

# Responses to Jay Strother
## Family-Equipping Ministry

## Response by Paul Renfro

Much in the family-equipping model encourages me. This model clearly understands the primacy of the home in the discipleship of the next generation. Its leadership is committed to equipping parents to disciple their children and to have families worship together. Parents and children serve side by side. Perhaps most important, the family-equipping model sees that family ministry is more than another set of programs added to an already-busy church calendar. Such commitment to bring reformation through an age-organized model is commendable.

### Three Important Questions

Still, as I look at the family-equipping model, I find myself asking three important questions: How do parents find time to disciple their children? How are men called to become the leaders? When and how are negligent parents to be confronted?

#### How Do Parents Find Time to Disciple Their Children?

It is truly encouraging to see a model that trains parents to disciple their children, even within age-segregated structures. And yet I wonder when these parents find time to disciple their children. Age-graded church activities are added to a calendar that typically includes two parents working, school, homework,

168 —

extracurricular activities, and school-based social events. Age-graded ministries segregate family members on Wednesdays and for Bible study on Sundays. And then there are the age-organized social events that inevitably grow out of age-segregated ministries.

Is the family-equipping model committed to downsizing the busy schedule that age-segregation programs typically produce? There are only so many hours and so much energy in a day. When days are filled with age-segregated social activities, family discipleship can quickly end up forgotten or tacked on the schedule after families have finished the church obstacle course. Family discipleship requires families to spend time together. It cannot be squeezed into the overcommitted, fragmented schedules to which age-segregated ministries have tended to contribute.

Does the family-equipping model call parents to evaluate the lifestyle choices that have overpacked their schedules in the first place? Jay Strother clearly sketched out the values of most parents as they pursue the materialistic American dream. In many church settings such lifestyles are seen as unavoidable. Yet these lifestyles need to be confronted by the Word of God, and parents must reevaluate their priorities in light of Scripture, especially their biblical responsibilities toward their children. Unless the family's schedules and priorities are reformed, church reformation will have little effect. Does the family-equipping church truly call members to have their schedules and priorities transformed in light of God's Word?

### How Are Men Called to Become the Leaders?

In the family-equipping model, I do not see a clear call for men to lead their families. I see the church leading in the plan to bring discipleship to homes. Yet who does God hold responsible for family discipleship? Throughout Scripture, God holds men accountable for the discipleship that takes place under their roofs (Deut 6; Ps 78; Eph 6:4). When Adam's household fell into sin, God first confronted Adam because he was responsible for training his family in God's Word.

Is the family-equipping model committed to restoring men to their biblical role as spiritual leaders in their homes? In the family-equipping model, ministers seem to be leading in the planning and implementation of family discipleship. Given the sad state of affairs in most Christian homes, this might appear helpful as a transitional phase. But when are the men fully entrusted to carry out their biblical responsibility? A man knows the difference between heading to the job site as a worker and as a foreman. As a foreman, he comes prepared to take charge; he develops a plan and acquires the tools to accomplish the task. As a worker, he simply waits to be told what to do. In the family-equipping model, fathers seem to have the role of workers, not the role of foremen.

Men must be weaned from their dependence on church programs so they will take charge of the discipleship occurring in their own homes. Young men must catch the vision of becoming leaders in their homes one day. In homes with single mothers, young men must be equipped to step into the shoes of leadership as early as fifteen or sixteen by serving and leading their families in worship. The apostle Paul admonished the first generation of Christian men to come out of paganism to bring up children "in the discipline and instruction of the Lord." Any man with the Holy Spirit and the Word of God can be equipped and expected to carry out this God-given duty.

### When and How Are Negligent Parents to Be Confronted?

The family equipping model reminds parents that they are the primary disciple-makers of their children and encourages parents in that task—that much is clear. But what does the church's leadership do when Christian parents refuse to disciple their children? Are family-equipping ministers willing to confront those who choose to live in blatant disobedience? What do you do with the parents who have not caught the vision for discipling their children?

It seems that proponents of family-equipping ministry simply hope that their leaders' warmth will challenge disconnected parents and that the oft-repeated expectations for family discipleship will somehow rub off on church members. I am sure that this works in some cases, but being a shepherd requires that we sometimes move beyond mere encouragement. Paul exhorted Timothy in 2 Tim 4:1–2: "Before God and Christ Jesus, who is going to judge the living and dead, . . . I solemnly charge you: . . . rebuke, correct, and encourage with great patience and teaching."

Because Jesus Christ is returning as the divine judge, pastors must call fathers and mothers to obey God's Word. For stubborn parents, reproof and rebuke may be necessary. In days gone by, fathers in Scotland were kept from the Lord's table when they neglected family discipleship. Are family-equipping churches willing and prepared to exercise church discipline when parents rebel against God by refusing to disciple their children?

### Incrementalism Versus Family Integration

Jay Strother acknowledges that the family-equipping model may require years to take root and to permeate every level of the church's life. I am grateful for this model because it *does* take great effort to retrain people and ministers who have been conditioned in age-segregated models. This work of retraining will, however, be especially difficult as long as age segregation remains in place. Progress will be slow because the majority will be comfortable with the *status quo* of age-graded ministry. Age-segregated ministry naturally works against the equipping of parents by enabling parents to continue abdicating their responsibility because their children are, after all, receiving *some* training from caring adult leaders, right?

Family integration completely removes the entire age-segregating structure and calls parents to begin discipling their children now. Parents who "get it" can jump right in. For parents who do not get it at first, the church's integrated culture, membership process, and the parents who do engage in family discipleship combine to provide an atmosphere of encouragement to let go of the past and to embrace biblical reform. On more than one occasion, we have seen first-time visitors—parents who had no previous thought of family discipleship—begin discipling their children the very next week!

### Clarifying What Is Meant by Family Integration

A family-integrated church does *not* claim, as some critics seem to suggest, that parents should serve as the sole disciple-makers in their children's lives. For us as for proponents of family-equipping ministry, discipleship is a joint venture between the church and family. Yet, in the family-integrated church, we recognize that age segregation is not necessary for discipleship to occur. Since so many of us have been raised by and trained for age-segregated ministry, it is easy to forget that age-segregation is the new kid on the block. It's been around less than a century, while age integration has been around for more than nineteen hundred years.

Family-integrated churches provide discipleship for children in at least three ways outside the home: First, through preaching and teaching in Sunday worship services, we confront children weekly with the truth of God's Word. Second, in small groups that entire families attend, we disciple not only parents but also children. Third, through relationships of the sort Paul described in Titus 2:1–8, children experience spiritual mentoring and modeling from more mature saints. Without age-segregation, there is more time to develop these sorts of mentoring relationships. Mentoring rounds out the discipleship that the parents provide. We do not deny that adults other than parents have significant roles to play in children's lives. Our position is simply that age-segregated instruction is unnecessary and, in many cases, counterproductive.

When it comes to children from broken or unbelieving families, what could be better than being "adopted" by a biblically functioning family? In this way the child's life intertwines not just with peers but with a family. The child experiences the blessing of Christian hospitality while observing firsthand Christian marriage, Christlike parenting, and the blessings and responsibilities of a Christian household. This pattern provides great vision and hope for the child's future.

I recall a young man whose mother's imprisonment had shattered his family. The father had abdicated his leadership role in the home. In the shadow of such a discouraging situation, our family "adopted" this young man for three years. We brought him to church each week; he sat with us in worship; we included him in our family's activities. He was like an older brother to our children. When we last heard from him, he was standing for Christ on his college campus, he had met a Christian girl, and they were considering marriage. This was the result of God's grace and a caring family—not of any age-segregated program.

Christian families are the primary disciple-makers in their children's lives, but Christian parents' divinely ordained responsibilities reach far beyond their own biological or adopted children to include those children whose lives the Lord has touched but whose parents are unable or unwilling to train their children in the Lord's ways.

The family-integrated model removes the middle man, the age-graded structure, that expends so much time and energy separating families. Family-integrated ministry restores the family as a context for ministry and training. We call men to embrace their leadership role. We deal directly with parents regarding their biblical responsibility to disciple their children. Once the age-segregated bubble is broken, reformation of families can happen quickly. Our simple schedules and structures provide families with the time they need to train their children, implicitly proclaiming God's command that parents are the primary disciple-makers in their children's lives.

One final benefit of family integration is that our structure is reproducible in any setting or culture, foreign or domestic. While I appreciate the great efforts of the family-equipping model to work within age-organized constraints, a family-equipping model would take years to implement—and this implementation would not be simple. As such, I must question the degree to which the family-equipping model is transferable and reproducible.

1

## *Response by Brandon Shields*

In one of my undergraduate psychology courses, the professor took us through a series of "optical illusions" to show how different people can perceive the same picture in different ways. My personal favorite was one where various perspectives revealed either a haggardly old woman with a big nose or a beautiful young woman wearing a bonnet. Some people saw the old woman first; others saw the younger woman more easily. This fascinating exercise demonstrated the power of perspective when it comes to how our brains analyze situations and people.

That illustration was the first thing that came to my mind as I considered the family-equipping model. It amazed me how two different groups of people—both dealing with the same issues and data—have arrived at completely different conclusions regarding the future of family ministry. The family-integrated model sees the challenges in the contemporary church and attempts to throw out all age-organized ministries; the family-equipping model sees the same difficulties yet seeks to build up families by overhauling age-appropriate ministry systems.

At so many levels, I find myself agreeing with the family-equipping approach. Specifically, I agree with how family-equipping ministers are:

- Championing both church and home in the process of reaching and discipling families
- Ruthlessly assessing ineffective ministry practices and initiating changes that involve both church leadership teams and parents
- Identifying ministry to young people as a priority in effective local church structures
- Engaging and supporting intact parental units through a well-organized and well-articulated process

There are, however, three aspects of family-equipping ministry that I would challenge: First, there is an insufficient rationale for embracing this approach. Second, the "strategic question" that seems to undergird family-equipping ministry is too lim-

O REORDER YOUR UPS DIRECT THERMAL LABELS:

. Access our supply ordering website at **UPS.COM**®
or contact UPS at 800-877-8652

. Please refer to Label # 01774006 when ordering.

01774006      RRD

Store Number: 634

Southeastern University Bookst
1000 Longfellow Boulevard
Lakeland, FL 33801
(863)667-5048

6340000046996 - 0008352198     08/17/2021

W00478603

Sandy Evans
1000 Longfellow Boulevard
Lakeland, FL 33801

*Shipping Mode: Ground*
*Questions about returns or items received, contact the bookstore or customer service at 1-888-279-8008.*

| ISBN | Title | DueDate |
|------|-------|---------|
| 9780805448450 | Perspectives on Family Ministry (B&H Pub) | |

ited. Finally, there appears to be no aggressive, missional posture toward the larger community.

## Lack of Sufficient Rationale

In reading this defense of family-equipping ministry, I was struck by the relative absence of compelling reasons for abandoning other models in favor of a family-equipping approach. The lack of any strong answer to this *why* question was curious in light of the author's more substantive approach to the questions of *what* and *how*.

Jay Strother noted that there are "significant cracks in our ministry contexts." Working from one study conducted by the National Study of Youth and Religion, he generalized that, despite how churches have invested in traditional ministry structures over the past thirty years, churched children and youth are growing up "less likely than ever before to have a biblical perspective on life." In response to this assertion, I would ask a few simple questions: Which churches? Which children and youth? Less likely than when? And how do you define a "biblical perspective on life"?

The author simply does not provide convincing evidence that churches or youth ministries are actually failing to equip parents to disciple their kids effectively. Maybe the problems the author observed in his own ministry setting were the result of a unique set of cultural circumstances. Maybe his church misappropriated otherwise good youth ministry principles. Or maybe there is really no sufficient or compelling rationale for discarding "traditional youth ministry" structures in favor of a family-equipping model.

## The "Strategic Question" Is Too Limited

Every ministry model must have a litmus test for defining and evaluating success. For some youth ministries, it is the sheer number of people present in the midweek program. Other churches measure effective discipleship by how many students were baptized that year and track year-to-year totals for comparison.

The family-equipping model is no different in this regard. It seems that the strategic question undergirding family-equipping ministry is, Is this God's best for families? From this, it appears that success in this model is measured by objective and subjective indicators that families are experiencing God's best at every level of the church's ministry.

This strategic question is certainly one aspect of a healthy philosophy of family ministry. Churches should provide parents with every possible resource for the task of discipling their children. Youth ministries failing to address this need, either in theory or in function, are forfeiting at least one part of the church's God-given mandate to equip the people of God. At a practical level these sorts of ministries typically see a law of diminishing returns—putting in more effort but receiving fewer results, putting in more time but having less influence.

Yet this question should be only one aspect of measuring healthy ministry. If the primary question we ask about our ministries always has to do with God's best for families, then by necessity we are not asking another equally valid question: "Is God's best *only* for our families?" If every aspect of the church's ministry is asking, "Is this God's best for families?" then the scope of the church's influence will be limited mostly to those families that are intact or that are currently "in the pipeline." Inevitably, churches engaged in this family-equipping model will spend most of their time and energy focusing on the needs of families. Such churches are likely to produce the most excellent family conferences, parent resources, catalytic venues, and family worship opportunities in the history of the church. But such a church falls far short of "God's best" because God's best is not limited to intact families. Single moms deserve to experience God's best. Kids with a father in jail deserve God's best. Children in foster care deserve God's best. The disenfranchised kid at the local public high school who would never set foot on church property deserves God's best. "Is this God's best for families?" is a good question to ask, but it is insufficient in itself.

## Lack of an Aggressive Missional Posture

The word *missional* has become an evangelical buzzword that has been the subject of much discussion in recent years. While I recognize that the phrase "becoming missional" is in danger of turning into a cliché, I simply mean "adopting the posture of a missionary, . . . being intentional and deliberate about reaching others."[1]

Throughout this defense of family-equipping ministry, I noticed a barrage of references to the church and the home, but there was a conspicuous scarcity of references to the community. This is my primary issue both with the family-integrated and family-equipping models. The result of actively promoting the family as the centerpiece of the church's mission is a built-in neglect of the larger community and of non-intact families present in the church. It is difficult to reach out aggressively in one's own ZIP code when most of the church's resources, energies, strategies, and leadership efforts have been targeted at intact families inside the church walls. As Chap Clark has noted, such an approach "will have virtually no impact on the missional calling of the church to disenfranchised, uninterested, and antagonistic young people. Most of these adolescents simply will not be drawn to a church congregation, even if it is a loving, caring, and inclusive family."[2]

Family-equipping ministers seem to assume that the primary goal of youth ministry should be to equip families to disciple their own children—but that's only partly correct. Another goal of youth ministry should be to fulfill the mandate of Jesus to be sent into the world as his witnesses (Matt 28:18–20; John 17; Acts 1:6–8). The historical impetus for youth ministry was a passionate desire in parachurch organizations—and eventually churches—to reach a youth culture that was hostile to the gospel. This outcome is only possible when churches, from top to bottom, choose to make aggressive community engagement a priority.

Jay Strother did list "to love to tell others about Jesus Christ and to share their own story of faith" as one of the six desired

1. E. Stetzer, *Planting Missional Churches* (Nashville, Tenn.: B&H, 2006), 19.
2. Clark, "Missional Approach," 29 (see chap. 3, n. 57).

outcomes for students. But how do students, parents, or the leadership team strategically accomplish this objective or determine whether it is being fulfilled? How can this model maintain an aggressive evangelistic posture when equipping families is such a central priority? How can family-equipping ministry truly be missional?

# Why Family-Equipping Ministry Still Works

## Jay Strother

In the preface to his classic work *The Screwtape Letters*, C. S. Lewis makes this observation: "There are two equal and opposite errors into which our race can fall about the devils. One is to disbelieve in their existence. The other is to believe, and to feel an excessive and unhealthy interest in them."[3] In the realm of spiritual warfare, Lewis wisely calls us to a carefully balanced life that avoids getting stuck in the "ditch" on either side of the road. I am convinced that our approach to family ministry must be every bit as carefully balanced and biblical as our approach to spiritual warfare. That is why I am so passionate about family-equipping ministry. Family-equipping ministry pursues a pathway avoiding the ditches that run along the extremities on either side of the path.

### Avoiding the Extremes

On one extreme the family-based ministry model downplays the real causes for alarm that have emerged in the past several

3. C. S. Lewis, *The Screwtape Letters* (San Francisco, Calif.: HarperCollins, 1942), ix.

RESPONSES TO JAY STROTHER — **179**

years as indicators that contemporary youth and children's ministries are not having a lasting spiritual impact. If not careful, family-based ministry may apply a Band-Aid where radical surgery is needed. A Band-Aid approach to family ministry is attempting to reconnect church and home with merely a ministry aimed at parents here, a father-son event there, and an intergenerational mission effort somewhere else.

Such attempts are laudable, but they will never be sufficient to change the hearts of parents who have abdicated their responsibility to serve as primary disciple-makers in their children's lives. To be sure, a handful of churches may seem to have succeeded while pursuing a family-based approach. Yet it is too easy in the family-based approach to ignore the fact that real crises of faith in many young lives can be traced to discipleship that never occurred at home.

On the other extreme the family-integrated approach focuses so much attention on traditional family structures that it would be easy to lose sight of God's heart for the broken, the lost, and the disenfranchised. While the Lord's ideal plan for children does include faith-nurturing family structures, he also calls his people to care for those in fractured and fragmented families. If not held in check, the family-integrated church could become more consumed with the ideal of being "a family of families" than with sharing the gospel of Jesus Christ.

## Is There Sufficient Warrant for the Change
## to Family-Equipping Ministry?

Standing squarely between these two approaches, the family-equipping model provides the most balanced and biblical response to the challenges that the church faces today in reconnecting the church and home.

Pressing for family-based ministry, Brandon Shields has questioned whether sufficient rationale exists for radical changes of the sort that family-equipping ministry requires. Specifically, he questions whether churched youth today are actually "less likely than ever before to have a biblical perspective on life." While alarmists who behave badly with statistics do exist in our midst, there are mounds of reliable research demonstrating that the current generation of children and youth is indeed "less likely than ever before to have a biblical perspective on life."

Christian Smith's recent study has demonstrated that the majority of churched teenagers today cannot even verbalize basic Christian beliefs, let alone articulate a Christ-centered worldview:

> When teenagers talked in their interviews about grace, they were usually talking about *Will and Grace,* not about God's grace. When teenagers discussed honor, they were almost always talking about honors courses or making the honor roll at school, very rarely about honoring God with their lives.[4]

A quick scan of other studies from the past few years echoes this same theme: "A biblical worldview in adults is presently declining even as spirituality remains hot."[5] "Busters and Mosaics are considerably less likely than previous generations to exhibit a biblical worldview,"[6] and "an acceptance of moral relativism is far higher among younger generations than older generations."[7]

Without a doubt, there are a few exceptional churches whose programmatic, age-graded ministries have consistently produced great men and women of God—though I have a suspicion the ministers leading nearly all of these congregations emphasized a strong home-church partnership long before it became a topic of popular discussion. These few notable exceptions cannot, however, counterbalance the growing mass of hard data and anecdotal evidence pointing to this single reality: *The programmatic, professionalized, age-segregated model that has dominated discipleship efforts in the past few decades is not working.* The very fact that a broad audience of pastors and seminary professors has been awaiting this particular book demonstrates that the people

---

4. Smith and Denton, *Soul Searching,* 167 (see chap. 5, n. 101).
5. www.barna.org/FlexPage.aspx?Page=BarnaUpdateNarrowPreview&BarnaUpdate ID=271.
6. www.barna.org/FlexPage.aspx?Page=BarnaUpdate&BarnaUpdateID=154.
7. www.barna.org/FlexPage.aspx?Page=BarnaUpdate&BarnaUpdateID=106.

who serve churches every week, and the leaders who train them, are not satisfied with the current return on their investments!

Convicted that the iceberg really is cracking, family-equipping pastors unashamedly ask a key strategic question in order to be part of the solution: "What is best for families?" Many churches today focus on strategic questions that count buildings, budgets, and bodies. Family-equipping congregations do not. Our conviction is that courageously asking one key strategic question—"What is best for families?"—in every aspect of church life helps us focus on numbers that represent a lasting difference: How many of our children and students will be living for God fifty years from now? How many church members are outstanding fathers who lead their homes or mothers who inspire and nurture their families? How many believers have we equipped for service and sent out from their neighborhoods to every place on the planet?

Certainly, some churches *will* twist "family ministry" into a self-serving array of programs and inwardly focused opportunities. This is not the fault of any particular family ministry model, however; this is the fault of poor leadership in these congregations.

Family-equipping churches understand that family ministry is an inherently missional endeavor. When God called Abraham and his family to trust in Divine Providence, missional calling and family discipleship were inextricably intertwined together so that "all the nations of the earth will be blessed through [Abraham]. For I have chosen him so that he will command his children and his house after him to keep the way of the LORD" (Gen 18:18–19). Thousands of years after God revealed his hidden counsels to Abraham, family-equipping churches recognize that the call for the church to evangelize the world and the call for parents to disciple their children still go hand in hand.

As family-equipping churches strengthen homes, it makes a difference not only in the lives of the parents but also in the lasting life of the community. A family-equipping focus does not isolate us from broken families but rather enables us to reach struggling parents and hurting children in our community. Why? Because we offer help, hope, and guidance for families, providing parents with better ways to raise their children. One member of our team put it this way: "Unbelieving parents don't lie awake at night worrying about their relationship with God; they lie awake at night worrying about their kids." The family-equipping model works precisely because it does *not* exclude single parents, children with a parent in jail, or disconnected teenagers. Instead, family-equipping ministry provides them with access to full participation in the faith community while modeling for them what a Christian home ought to look like.

Family-equipping churches continually reinforce the missional nature of their ministry as they challenge families to serve together, both through local mission projects and through large-scale mission journeys. In the coming year our particular family-equipping congregation will launch a new campus in one of the fastest-growing communities in the nation, a community where children under the age of four represent the largest population group! Why? Our emphasis on church-home partnership has helped us see that, instead of simply building bigger and better facilities at our current location, we must impact and equip more families by moving beyond our walls to reach them.

## Calling Leaders and Parents to Obedience

So much in the church rises or falls with authentic spiritual leadership. The team that is entrusted with leading a church to reengage the home must muster the courage to eliminate the endless schedules of programs and events that age-graded churches typically offer. That is partly why the family-equipping model focuses on strategies instead of the stream of programs and events that characterizes family-based and programmatic congregations. Parents must be provided time to spend with their families while still receiving the tools they need to disciple their children.

Spiritual leadership in a family-equipping church also includes calling men to leadership in their homes and in the church. Family-equipping churches equip men for their God-ordained role by coordinating every aspect of ministry—from worship celebrations to discipleship groups and mission opportunities—to develop God-honoring family relationships. The leadership in a family-equipping congregation embraces the same responsibility as the leaders in a family-integrated church, which is calling parents to obedience and, when necessary, to repentance. The key is to speak the truth in love (Eph 4:15). When Christian parents become aware of a leader's deep love for them, they become open to accountability and correction.

## Family-Equipping Ministry: Reproducible and Transferable

Despite the many strengths of family-integrated ministry, I respectfully disagree with Paul Renfro's assertion that the family-integrated model is reproducible in any culture. The vast majority of evangelical churches still see kingdom value in biblically focused, age-organized ministries. In most such churches, movement into a family-integrated approach would tear the congregation apart.

While there are challenges in transitioning a church to a family-equipping model, such transitions are part of the leader's calling to shepherd the people entrusted to his care and to help them navigate the choppy waters of transition. Given the broad gap between the family-integrated approach and the present predicament of most churches, I remain firmly convicted that the family-equipping approach is the most transferable and reproducible model because it can be applied in any setting and have an impact resonating throughout the entire culture of the church.

## The Changing Conversation

The conversation in churches throughout North America is beginning to change. The energy expended in the past figuring out how to attract greater numbers of children and students to our events is slowly giving way to questions of greater consequence. The fact that this book is now being read demonstrates a quiet revolution gaining momentum at the grassroots level. Everywhere I turn and travel, the best leaders are asking how we can give our lives away to raise up a generation of men and women who love God and are emboldened by the Holy Spirit to spread the hope of Jesus to the nations. Inevitably, my discussions with these leaders turn to the subject of parents and to the challenge of reengaging families in worship, discipleship, and missional living.

In the critically acclaimed work *The Great Emergence*, Phyllis Tickle points out that, every half millennium or so, the Holy Spirit compels the church to hold "a giant rummage sale." The reforms that occur as a result of this ecclesiastical rummage sale have a remarkable effect: existing institutions are purified, fresh expressions of faith emerge, and the message of Christianity reaches more people than ever before.[8]

Phyllis Tickle's conviction is that we are living in one such period of history right now, and I am convinced she is right. I am further convinced that one critical component of this new reformation will be a renewed emphasis on home-church partnership. Practitioners and professors such as Mark DeVries, Richard Ross, and Reggie Joiner began to sound the call a few years ago. Now the people responsible for training the next generation of ministers—ranging from Ben Freudenburg and Chap Clark to Randy Stinson and Timothy Paul Jones—are developing diverse models of family ministry to enable congregations throughout North America to do church in radically different ways.

The culture has spent much of the past century attacking the institution of the family. In many cases the church has acquiesced. But God is now raising a generation of leaders seeking to restore the power, vitality, and importance of the church-home partnership. What our Enemy has meant for evil, God will use for good. As increasing numbers of families continue to be fractured and fragmented, Christ-centered families will stand out more and more as outposts of light in neighborhoods of darkness.

My fellow authors and I differ on some significant points when it comes to how this is best carried out at the level of the local church. Yet we stand in agreement that ministry to families is essential kingdom work and that this work must rank with our highest priorities. It is such an exciting time to enter this great conversation! I look forward to how the Spirit will continue

---

8. P. Tickle, *The Great Emergence: How Christianity Is Changing and Why* (Grand Rapids, Mich.: Baker, 2008), 16–17.

to shape and grow this movement, with "iron sharpening iron" as more leaders join the effort. Consider this book a personal invitation to join God as He stirs the hearts of leaders in His churches!

# Author Index

Adams, D. . . . . . . . . . . . . . . . . . . . .117
Alexander, J. . . . . . . . . . . . . . . 69, 70
Anthony, M. . . . . . . . . .18, 20, 44, 52
Arnett, J. . . . . . . . . . . . . . . . . . . . .115
Arterburn, S. . . . . . . . . . . . . . . . .132

Bakke, O. M. . . . . . . . . . . . . . . . . .18
Balla, P. . . . . . . . . . . . . . . . . . . . . .157
Barna, G. . . . . . . . . . . . . 47, 102–103
Baucham, V. . . . 55–56, 56, 80, 100,
    102, 106, 113, 123–124
Baxter, R. . . . . . . . . . . . . 65, 126–127
Bennett, N. . . . . . . . . . . . . . . . . . . .26
Benson, W. . . . . . . . . . . . . . . . . . . .18
Black, D. . . . . . . . . . . . . . . . . 60, 61
Block, D. . . . . . . . . . . . . . . . . . . . .157
Bredfeldt, G. . . . . . . . . . . . . . . . . . .32
Burns, J. . . . . . . . . . . . . . . . . . . . . .98
Burrell, B. . . . . . . . . . . . . . . . . . . . .29
Bushell, M. . . . . . . . . . . . . . . . . . .112

Cannister, M. . . . . . . . . . . . . . . . . .29
Chesterton, G. K. . . . . . . . . . . . . . .47
Clark, C. . . . . 11–12, 33, 34, 37–39,
    52, 177, 184
Clowney, E. . . . . . . . . . . . . . . . . . .134
Comenius, J. . . . . . . . . . . . . . . 30, 31
Coontz, S. . . . . . . . . . . . . . . . . . . . .31

Dallimore, A. . . . . . . . . . . . . . . . . .160
Davies, H. . . . . . . . . . . . . . . . . . . .160
Demos, J. . . . . . . . . . . . . . . . . . . . .28
Denton, M. . . . . . .67, 126, 141, 180
DeVries, M. . . . .9, 32, 37, 43–45, 52,
    98, 99, 127, 130
Dewey, J. . . . . . . . . . . . . . . . . 30–31
Drazin, N. . . . . . . . . . . . . . . . . . . . .18

Eckelberry, R. . . . . . . . . . . . . . . . . .29
Edwards, J. . . . . . . . . . . . . . . .21–22
Erb, F. . . . . . . . . . . . . . . . . . . . . . . .29

Felton, J. . . . . . . . . . . . . . . . . . . . . .132

Frame, J. . . . . . . . . . . . . . . . . . . . . .112

Freudenberg, B. . . . . . . . . . . . 44, 52

Garland, D. . . . . . . . . . . . . . . . . . . .38

Geiger, E.. . . . . . . . . . . . . . . . .84–85

Graves, C. . . . . .44, 49, 52, 101, 144

Greenway, R. . . . . . . . . . . . . . . . . . .64

Grenz, J. . . . . . . . . . . . . . . . . . . . . .11

Hall, G. S. . . . . . . . . . . . . . . . 27, 30

Hall, S. . . . . . . . . . . . . . . . 107, 114

Halper, D. . . . . . . . . . . . . . . . . . . .31

Hemphill, K. . . . . . . . . . . . . 147, 148

Hersch, P. . . . . . . . . . . . . . . . 32, 48

Hine, T. . . . . . . . . . . . . . . . . . . . . .114

House, P. . . . . . . . . . . . . . . 125, 132

Joiner, R. . . . . . . . . . . . . . . . . . . . .149

Keillor, S. . . . . . . . . . . . . . . . . 28, 32

Kett, J. . . . . . . . . . . . . . . . . . . 27, 30

King, M. . . . . . . . . . . . . . . . .101–102

Kirn, W. . . . . . . . . . . . . . . . . . .27–28

Köstenberger, A. . . . . . . . . . .158–159

Kotter, J. . . . . . . . . . . . . . . . .140–141

Kubiak, K. . . . . . . . . . . . . . . . . . . .102

Lawson, K. . . . . . . . . . . . . . . . . . . .18

Lee, V. . . . . . . . . . . . . . . . . . .103–104

Lewis, C. S. . . . . . . . . . . . . . . . . . .178

Longman, T. III . . . . . . . . . . . . . . .158

Luther, M. . . . . . . . . . . . . . . . . . . .160

Lynn, R. . . . . . . . . . . . . . . . . . . . . .22

Mann, H. . . . . . . . . . . . . . . . . . . . .29

Marcellino, J. . . . . . . . . . . . . . . . . .69

Marsden, G. . . . . . . . . . . . . . . . . . .160

McNeil, R. . . . . . . . . . . . . . . . . . . .156

Mead, M. . . . . . . . . . . . . . . . . . . . .32

Mohler, A. . . . . . . . . . . . . . . . . . . .115

Monsma, T. . . . . . . . . . . . . . . . . . . .64

Mueller, W. . . . . . . . . . . . . . . . . . .111

Murrow, D. . . . . . . . . . . . . . . . . . . .85

Nel, M. . . . . . . . . . . . . . . . . . . 42, 52

Nielsen, R. . . . . . . . . . . . . . . . . . . .16

Offer, D. . . . . . . . . . . . . . . . . . . . . .30

Palladino, G. . . . . . . . . . . . . . . . . . .30

Palmer, E. . . . . . . . . . . . . . . . . . . . .99

Pancoast, D. . . . . . . . . . . . . . . . . . .38

Penner, M. . . . . . . . . . . . . . . . . . . .35

Pinckney, T. C. . . . . . . . . . . . . . . .103

Pipes, J. . . . . . . . . . . . . . . . . .103–104

Pipher, M. . . . . . . . . . . . . . . . . . . .48

Powell, K. . . . . . . . . . . . . . . . . . . .102

Prevost, R. . . . . . . . . . . . . . . . . . . .18

Rahn, D. . . . . . . . . . . . . . . . . . . . . .52

Rainer, T. . . . . . . . . . 84–85, 115–116

Rathgeber, H. . . . . . . . . . . . . . . . .140

Ray, B. . . . . . . . . . . . . . . . . . . . . . .93

Reed, J. . . . . . . . . . . . . . . . . . . . . .18

Reese, W. . . . . . . . . . . . . . . . . . . . .29

Reid, A. . . . . . . . . . . . . . 91, 101, 136

Robbins, A. . . . . . . . . . . . . . . . . . . .33

Robbins, D. . . . . . . . . . . . . . . . . . . .34

Ross, R. . . . . . .12, 127, 132, 147, 148

Rothbard, M. . . . . . . . . . . . . . . . . . .29

Sanchez, E. . . . . . . . . . . . . . . . . . .157

Scroggins, J. . . . . . . . . . . . . . . . . .117

Senter, M. III. . . . . . . . . 33, 114–115

Shields, B. . . . . . . . . . . . . . .104–106

Smith, C..66, 67, 126, 141–142, 180

Spurgeon, C. . . . . . . . . . . . . 136, 137

Stamps, D. L. . . . . . . . . . . . . . . .159

Stanley, A. . . . . . . . . . . . . . 107, 114

Steptoe, S. . . . . . . . . . . . . . . . . .108

Stetzer, E. . . . . . . . . . . . . . . . . .177

Strack, J. . . . . . . . . . . . . . . .103–104

Strange, W. A. . . . . . . . . 18, 159–160

Tickle, P. . . . . . . . . . . . . . . . . . .184

Walsh, D. . . . . . . . . . . . . . . . . . . .26

Wells, D. . . . . . . . . . 76–77, 122–123

West, D. . . . . . . . . . . . . . . . . . . . .26

Wilner, A.. . . . . . . . . . . . . . . . . . .33

Wishall, G.. . . . . . . . . . . . . . . . . .20

Wright, C. . . . . . . . . . . . . . . . . . .157

Wright, E. . . . . . . . . . . . . . . . 22, 24

Wright, S. . . . . .44, 49, 52, 101, 144

Yaconelli, M. . . . . . . . . . 24, 34, 101

Zorba, W.. . . . . . . . . . . . . . . . . . .34

# Subject Index

## A

accommodation . . . . . . . . . . . . . . 110
activity-driven ministry . . . . 108–109
adolescence . . . . . 26–28, 30, 32, 60,
    87
adult leaders . . . . . . . . . . . . . . . . . 154
age-integration . . . . . . . . 62–63, 68
age-organized ministry . . . 101–102,
    105–107, 111–113, 111–114,
    117, 137, 144, 162, 168
age segregation . . . . . . . . . . . 12, 14,
    16, 21–22, 24, 48, 55, 68, 70,
    74, 82, 91–92, 95–96, 100–101,
    122, 124, 169, 171–173, 180
age-specific ministers . . . . 12–13, 23

## B

biblical worldview . . . . . . . . 164, 180
burn out . . . . . . . . . . . . . . . . . . . . 163
business model church . . . . . 163–164

## C

catalysts . . . . . . . . . . . 149–156, 167
catechism . . . . . . . . . . . . . . . . . . . . 58
celebrities . . . . . . . . . . . . . . . . . . . . 33
character . . . . . . . . . . . . . . . . . . . . . 66
children . . . . . . . . . . . . . . . . . . . . . 148
    minister to . . . . . . . . . . . . . . . . . 131
    training of . . . . . . . . . . . . . . . . . . 75
    in worship service . . . . . . . . . 75–76
church . . . . . . . . . . . . . . . . . . . . . . 146
    as family . . . . 2–4, 38–39, 79–80,
    89
    New Testament . . . . . . . . . . . . . . 80
church attendance . . . . . . . . . . . . 128
church discipline . . . . . . . . . 170–171
compassion . . . . . . . . . . . . . . . . . . 116
*cultura et Scriptura* . . . . . . . . . . 122
cultural relevance . . . . . . . . . 121–122
culturally-immersed
    ministry . . . . . . . . . . . . . 110–111
curriculum . . . . . . . . . . . . . . . . . . 156

# D

discipleship . . . . . . . . 15, 63–64, 108
    family . . . . . . 19, 64–65, 137–138,
      158, 169
    joint venture . . . . . . . . . . . . . . .172
    men leading families . . . . .169–170
    New Testament . . . . . . . . .158–159
    through partnership with
      parents . . . . . . . . . . . . . . . . . .147
discipline . . . . . . . . . . . . . . . . . . . . .63
dropout statistic . . . . . . . . . .101–106

# E

ecclesiology . . . . . . . . . . . . . . 80, 135
education
    equal . . . . . . . . . . . . . . . . . . . . . .29
    public . . . . . . . . . . . . . . . . . 31, 114
80/20 rule . . . . . . . . . . . . . . . . . . . .87
elders . . . . . . . . . . . . . . . . . . . . .65–66
emerging generations . . . . 145, 161
evangelism . . . . . 63–64, 73, 80, 83,
    90, 114, 121, 124, 126
    of children . . . . . . . . . . . . . . . . .136
    of youth . . . . . . . . . . . . . . 125, 136
exfamization . . . . . . . . . . . . . . . . . .99

# F

family-based church . . . . . . . . . . .100
family-based ministry . . . .43, 44–45,
    52, 70, 98–120, 121–139,
    178–179
family-equipping ministry . . . 43–45,
    45, 52, 87–88, 127, 131–132,
    140–167, 144–145, 168–185

family-integrated ministry . . . 42–43,
    45, 52, 54–78, 79–82, 83–91,
    89–92, 94–97, 117, 123, 125,
    136, 138, 171–173, 177, 179,
    183
family ministry . . . . . . . . . . . 24, 184
    definition of . . . . . . . . . . . . . .40–41
    foundations of . . . . . . . . . . . .37–52
    missional endeavor . . . . . . . . . .181
    models for . . . . . . . . . . . . . . .41–52
    reasons for . . . . . . . . . . . . . . . .1–4
    terms for . . . . . . . . . . . . . . . . . .35
family of families . . . . . . 89–90, 179
family time . . . . . . . . . . . . . . . . . . .49
fathers . . . . . . . . .1, 17, 83, 158, 170
    faith of . . . . . . . . . . . . . . . . . . . .85
    hearts of . . . . . . . . . . . . . . . . . . .19
    Jewish . . . . . . . . . . . . . . . . . . . .18
    Old Testament . . . . . . . . . .157–158
    responsibility of . . . . . .2–4, 46–47,
      65, 67–69, 159
fellowship . . . . . . . . . . . . . . . .58–59
flexibility . . . . . . . . . . . 98, 128–129

# G

gender segregation . . . . . . . . . . . . .83
generational gap . . . . . . . . . . . 32, 34
generations . . . . . . 47–49, 109, 145–
    146, 157
"going native" . . . . . . . . . . . . . . . .111
Great Commission . . . 116–117, 135

# H

happiness . . . . . . . . . . . . . . .147–148
home school . . . . . . . . . . . 76, 76–78
hospitality . . . . . . . . . . . . . . 64, 172

husbands................. 1, 74
   responsibilities of ...........2–4

**I**
incrementalism.......... 164, 171
Industrial Revolution....27–28, 29, 114
intentionality ................138

**J**
Jesus, early training of.........159

**L**
leadership
   biblical..................65–66
   church................ 65, 163
   home as training ground ......66
   male.....................182
LifeGroup ...................152
lifestyle of worship ....... 132, 169
Lord's Supper ................58

**M**
manhood, biblical.......60–61, 72, 75, 116
market-driven churches.........76
marketing .................32–33
membership covenant ..........64
mentoring...................172
missional....................177
missions ...................153
mission statements.............16
moral therapeutic deism .......141

**N**
nontraditional families..........86
nuclear-family perspective ......39, 80–81

**P**
parachurch organizations ....33–34
parents
   disciple-makers.............162
   equipping of ...... 44, 106, 121, 126, 131, 145, 149, 168
   partnering with........ 145–148, 150–151
   responsibility of.......12–13, 16, 22–25, 34–35, 40–41, 47, 106
pastors....................65–66
preaching ............... 58, 172
programmatic ministry model....52

**R**
regulative principle .......112–113
relevance....................110
resource guide ...............151
rods......................75–76

**S**
schools
   high school ............. 27, 30
   home ............ 76, 82, 92–94
   public.....29, 30, 76, 81–82, 84, 92–94
Scripture......... 46, 77, 80, 112, 121–122
sexual revolution .............115
*shanan* .....................151
single-parent homes....... 86, 116
singles................ 71–72, 86
small groups......... 59, 158, 172
*sola cultura* ........ 122–123, 134
*sola Scriptura* ..... 122–124, 133–135

spiritual formation . . . . . 17, 22, 25,
    40–41, 47
Spiritual Formation Model for
    Emerging Generations . . . . .148
subculture. . . . . . . . . . . . . . . . . . .33
synagogues . . . . . . . . . . . . . . . .18–19

**T**
teenagers. . . . 24, 61, 66–67, 79, 86,
    115, 137, 180
therapeutic counseling. . . . . . . . . .38
tradition . . . . . . . . . . . . . . . . . . . .162

**U**
uni-generational ministry . .109–110

**W**
wives . . . . . . . . . . . . . . . . . . . . .74–75
worship . . . . . . 56–57, 64, 134–135,
    153–154

family. . . . . . . . . . . . . . 65, 70, 165
    in Old Testament . . . . . . . . . . . .69

**Y**
Young Life. . . . . . . . . . . . . . 9, 33–34
youth culture . . . . . . . . . . . . . . . .32
Youth for Christ . . . . . . . . . . . .33–34
youth groups. . . . . . . . . . . . . . . . .88
youth ministers . . . . . . . . . 109, 131
    frustrations of . . . . . . . . . . . . . .108
    tenure of . . . . . . . . . . . . . . . . . . .11
youth ministry . . 99, 122, 127, 130,
    176–177
    criticisms of. . . . . . . . . . . .100–101
    dynamic. . . . . . . . . . . . . . . . . . .105
    roots of . . . . . . . . . . . . . . . . . . .114
"youth problem". . . . . . . . . . . . . .114

# Scripture Index

**Genesis**
3:1 . . . . . . . . . . . . . . . . . . . . . . . . . .1
8:16–20 . . . . . . . . . . . . . . . . . . . . .69
17:8–9 . . . . . . . . . . . . . . . . . . . . .157
18:18–19 . . . . . . . . . . . . . . . . . . .181
18:19 . . . . . . . . . . . . . . . . . . 17, 68

**Exodus**
12:3 . . . . . . . . . . . . . . . . . . . . . . .157
12:21 . . . . . . . . . . . . . . . . . . . . . .157
12:25–28 . . . . . . . . . . . . . . . . . . .17
12:26–27 . . . . . . . . . . . . . . . . . .157
13:13–15 . . . . . . . . . . . . . . . . . .157
18. . . . . . . . . . . . . . . . . . . . . . . . . .87
22:22 . . . . . . . . . . . . . . . . . . . . . .116

**Leviticus**
19:32 . . . . . . . . . . . . . . . . . . . . . . .49

**Deuteronomy**
6 . . . . . . . . . . . . . . . . . . . . . . . . . .169
6:4–9 . . . . . . . . . . . . . . . . . . . . . .157
6:6–7 . . . . . . . . . . . . . . . . . . . . . . .17
6:7 . . . . . . . . . . . . . . 150, 151, 167

6:12 . . . . . . . . . . . . . . . . . . . . . . . .17
6:20–25 . . . . . . . . . . . . . . . . . . . .157
11:1–12 . . . . . . . . . . . . . . . . . . . . .17
29:10–11 . . . . . . . . . . . . . . . . . . . .62
31:12 . . . . . . . . . . . . . . . . . . . .49, 68

**Joshua**
4:5–7 . . . . . . . . . . . . . . . . . . . . . .157
8:35 . . . . . . . . . . . . . . . . . . . . . . . .62

**Judges**
2:10–12 . . . . . . . . . . . . . . . . . . . .158

**1 Samuel**
2:12–3:14. . . . . . . . . . . . . . . . . . .158
4:11–22 . . . . . . . . . . . . . . . . . . . .158
8:1–9 . . . . . . . . . . . . . . . . . . . . . .158

**2 Chronicles**
20:13 . . . . . . . . . . . . . . . . . . . . . . .62

**Ezra**
10:1 . . . . . . . . . . . . . . . . . . . . . . . .69

**Psalms**
68:5 . . . . . . . . . . . . . . . . . . . . . . . .86

71:17–18 . . . . . . . . . . . . . . . . . . . .167
78. . . . . . . . . . . . . . . . . . . . . . 68, 169
78:2–4 . . . . . . . . . . . . . . . . . . . . . . .18
78:5–6 . . . . . . . . . . . . . . . . . . . . . . .46
78:6–7 . . . . . . . . . . . . . . . . . . . . . . .18
127. . . . . . . . . . . . . . . . . . . . . . . . . .81

**Proverbs**

1:8 . . . . . . . . . . . . . . . . . 18, 49, 158
3:1 . . . . . . . . . . . . . . . . . . . . . . . . .49
4:1–4 . . . . . . . . . . . . . . . . . . . . . .158
6:20 . . . . . . . . . . . . . . . . . . . 49, 158
13:20 . . . . . . . . . . . . . . . . . . . 62, 94
13:24 . . . . . . . . . . . . . . . . . . . . . . .75
22:6 . . . . . . . . . . . . . . . . . . . 75, 158
22:15 . . . . . . . . . . . . . . . . . . . . . . .75
23:13 . . . . . . . . . . . . . . . . . . . . . . .75
29:15 . . . . . . . . . . . . . . . . . . . . . . .75

**Ecclesiastes**

1:9 . . . . . . . . . . . . . . . . . . . . . . . .157

**Jeremiah**

49:11 . . . . . . . . . . . . . . . . . . . . . .116

**Joel**

2:16 . . . . . . . . . . . . . . . . . . . . . . . .62

**Malachi**

4:6 . . . . . . . . . . . . . . . . . . . 2, 40, 63

**Matthew**

6:9 . . . . . . . . . . . . . . . . . . . . . . . . . .3
10:34–36 . . . . . . . . . . . . . . . . . . . .81
10:34–37 . . . . . . . . . . . . . . . . . . . .90
12:50 . . . . . . . . . . . . . . . . . . . . . .158
14:21 . . . . . . . . . . . . . . . . . . . . . .128
28:18–20 . . . . . . . . . . . . . . 116, 177

**Mark**

3:33–35 . . . . . . . . . . . . . . . . . . . . .81
10:14 . . . . . . . . . . . . . . . . . . . . . .120
10:45 . . . . . . . . . . . . . . . . . 150, 151
12:28–34 . . . . . . . . . . . . . . . . . . .145

**Luke**

1:17 . . . . . . . . . . . . . . . . . . . . 19, 40
2:44 . . . . . . . . . . . . . . . . . . . . . . .159
2:46 . . . . . . . . . . . . . . . . . . . . . . . .60

**John**

6:66 . . . . . . . . . . . . . . . . . . . . . . .128
17. . . . . . . . . . . . . . . . . . . . . . . . .177

**Acts**

1:6–8 . . . . . . . . . . . . . . . . . . . . . .177
1:8 . . . . . . . . . . . . . . . . . . . . . . . .116
2:39 . . . . . . . . . . . . . . . . . . . . . . .159
2:46 . . . . . . . . . . . . . . . . . . . . . . . .58
6. . . . . . . . . . . . . . . . . . . . . . . . . .164
6:1–7 . . . . . . . . . . . . . . . . . . . . . . .87
10. . . . . . . . . . . . . . . . . . . . . . . . .125
11:14 . . . . . . . . . . . . . . . . . . . . . .159
16. . . . . . . . . . . . . . . . . . . . . . . . .125
16:1 . . . . . . . . . . . . . . . . . . . . . . . .62
16:15 . . . . . . . . . . . . . . . . . . . . . . .64

**Romans**

8. . . . . . . . . . . . . . . . . . . . . . . . . . .80
8:15 . . . . . . . . . . . . . . . . . . . . . . . . .3
10:14–15 . . . . . . . . . . . . . . 150, 151
12. . . . . . . . . . . . . . . . . . . . . . . . . .80
12:1–2 . . . . . . . . . . . . 132, 150, 151

**1 Corinthians**

1:16 . . . . . . . . . . . . . . . . . . . . . . . .64
1:23–29 . . . . . . . . . . . . . . . . . . . . .49
9:22–23 . . . . . . . . . . . . . . . 116, 123

12.......................80, 81

12:13........................49

**Galatians**

3:28.........................49

4:1–7........................80

6:10.........................64

**Ephesians**

1:4–6........................80

2:14.........................49

4............................164

4:4–7.................150, 151

4:11–13......................81

4:15.........................183

6............................81

6:1–3..................69, 159

6:1–4........................63

6:4..........19, 47, 68, 159, 169

**Philippians**

4:9..........................66

**Colossians**

3............................81

3:11.........................49

3:20...................69, 159

3:21.........................19

3:23.........................68

**1 Thessalonians**

2:11–12......................19

**1 Timothy**

1:2..........................62

3:4.....................62, 66

3:15.........................80

4:7–12................150, 151

4:12.........................61

**2 Timothy**

1:2..........................62

1:15........................159

3:15–17...............150, 151

4:1–2.......................171

4:19...................42, 55

**Titus**

1:6.....................62, 66

2:1–8......59, 62, 77, 88, 96, 109, 172

**Hebrews**

12:5–11.......................3

**James**

1:27...................86, 116

5:14–16......................58

**1 Peter**

4:17.........................80